D1449361

A
WORD
A
DAY

—

**365 Words
to Augment Your
Vocabulary**

Also by Joseph Piercy

∽

THE 25 RULES OF GRAMMAR

∽

1000 WORDS TO ENHANCE YOUR
VOCABULARY

∽

A
WORD
A
DAY

—

365 Words
to Augment Your
Vocabulary

JOSEPH PIERCY

Michael O'Mara Books Limited

First published in Great Britain in 2019 by
Michael O'Mara Books Limited
9 Lion Yard
Tremadoc Road
London SW4 7NQ

A CIP catalogue record for this book is available from the British Library.

Papers used by Michael O'Mara Books Limited are natural, recyclable
products made from wood grown in sustainable forests. The
manufacturing processes conform to the environmental regulations
of the country of origin.

ISBN: 978-1-78929-163-6 in hardback print format
ISBN: 978-1-78929-167-4 in ebook format

1 2 3 4 5 6 7 8 9 10

Designed and typeset by K.DESIGN, Winscombe, Somerset
Printed and bound by CPI Group (UK) Ltd, Croydon, CR0 4YY

www.mombooks.com

Introduction: The Problem with Definitions

'The most valuable of all talents is that of never using two words when one will do.'

THOMAS JEFFERSON

'So difficult it is to show the various meanings and imperfections of words when we have nothing else but words to do it with.'

JOHN LOCKE

'Lexicographer: a writer of dictionaries; a harmless drudge that busies himself in tracing the original and detailing the signification of words.'

SAMUEL JOHNSON

In the preface to his famous *Dictionary of the English Language* (1755), Samuel Johnson writes of 'the energetic unruliness of the English tongue'. Johnson's dictionary had been commissioned by a group of London booksellers with the purpose of providing a definitive lexicography of English. Johnson accepted the commission, partly due to the money on offer and to satisfy his considerable intellectual ego, but mainly because the English language was in dire need of some sort of order. 'Wherever I turned,' Johnson wrote, 'there was perplexity to be disentangled, and confusion to be regulated.' Johnson's dictionary took eight years to compile (with the help of eight research assistants) and contained over 40,000 words – this sounds like a long time, but the comparable dictionary of French published in the same era took a team of scholars fifty-five years to compile. However, in his final revised edition of 1773, Johnson partly concedes that his attempt to 'fix' the meaning of words had been impossible to wholly achieve.

Johnson had recognized that language is fluid and always in a state of flux. Rather than setting meaning in stone to impose order on the 'energetic unruliness', as he had hoped, Johnson was in fact merely recording the meaning of words as they were in his day. This is the problem that lexicographers (compilers of dictionaries) face: if meaning fluctuates from epoch to epoch, does it not follow that any definition of a word in 2019 may have changed to something quite notably different by 2219? Possibly. Yet not all words change their meaning and it would be dangerous to believe that anything goes when it comes to language. One of the mysteries I tried to unravel when compiling this book was how it is that certain words change their meaning over time whereas others remain more or less fixed.

Of the three principle parts of speech, adjectives and verbs are the most susceptible to subtle shifts in meaning. Nouns stay pretty much the same. Problems start to occur with words that have dual meanings – for example the word 'fathom', which can be both a noun and a verb. Fathom originates from the Old English word *fæthm*, which meant 'outstretched arms'. A fathom as a noun was a measurement from fingertip to fingertip. As a verb, fathom meant to encircle something with one's arms, embrace or hug. When people wanted to know how deep a body of water was they measured it in fathoms (roughly six feet), used sounding lines (a weighted rope marked in fathoms) and drew fathom lines on nautical charts to record the information. At this point the meaning of embracing something disappeared and to fathom meant to measure depth. Over time, this notion of measuring depth took on a subsidiary meaning when used figuratively to 'get to the bottom' of some problem or conundrum, to metaphorically 'fathom it out'. Fathom is a good example of how the meaning of words moves in subtle directions according to changes in human life and civilization. Before technology in seafaring developed rapidly in the late medieval period, people would use fathom to mean giving each other a cuddle.

Words give shape to our world; they also allow us to create stories and myths and these stories feed back into the language in other ways. Take the word 'clue', meaning a piece of evidence that leads to the solution of a problem. The word clue was originally spelled *clew* and signified a ball of yarn or thread. By the mid-seventeenth century, however, it had come to mean a method to resolve a mystery. Why? The answer lies in Greek mythology. Theseus escapes from the Minotaur and his impossible maze by unravelling a ball of thread and retracing his steps. So when people speak of finding 'clues to unravel a mystery' they are inadvertently referencing the story of Theseus and the Minotaur.

Similar stories emerge from behind words such as tantalize and mercurial. Historical figures, rightly or wrongly, are immortalized in words such as tawdry, gerrymander and nepotism. I have tried, where possible, to include a broad spread of words, some rare and archaic, some which are often mistaken or misused and some where the meaning has evolved over time. New words are added to the English language all the time – Xertz, for example, the origin of which is unclear, but possibly derives from slang German and drinking games during October beer festivals. To xertz, in case you were wondering, is to greedily gulp down a drink. The last word in this list is serendipity, which I chose because, in a way, it has summed up my feelings when compiling this book. I often found that when researching the origins or development of a particular word I would inadvertently stumble across others, a most serendipitous process tracing meanings that spiral away into different directions. It is my hope that readers will experience serendipity when browsing through this miscellaneous lexicography.

Joseph Piercy

1 Imbroglio

NOUN

A curious word that is closely linked to the transitive verb embroil, meaning to involve someone (or oneself) in a dispute or conflict. Imbroglio as a noun is slightly more sinister and suggests something underhand is going on, such as a public scandal or social faux pas that the participants would rather not be embroiled in.

> *The imbroglio in which he found himself entwined was wholly of his own making.*

❧

2 Petard

NOUN

A petard is a small bomb in the form of a metal receptacle filled with compacted gunpowder and a fuse. Dating from the sixteenth-century Middle French, petards were traditionally used to blow open doors and gateways to fortifications during battles. Some etymologists, perhaps with their tongues in their cheeks, have noted that petard has links to the Latin word *pedere*, meaning 'to break wind', which is the base for the French word *peter*, to fart. The word is best known in English for the phrase 'hoist with his own petard' from Shakespeare's *Hamlet*. In the play, Hamlet is to be sent to England with his two hapless companions, Rosencrantz and Guildenstern, who carry a letter requesting Hamlet's execution. Shakespeare scholars have debated how exactly Hamlet knew the content of the 'sealed' letter, with some suggesting it is a plot hole (narrative error). However, other critics point out that a lot of action occurs offstage in *Hamlet* (Ophelia's descent into madness and suicide being a prime example). The phrase has come to be applied to someone undone by their own actions and follies.

> *There's letters sealed; and my two schoolfellows,*
> *Whom I will trust as I will adders fanged,*
> *They bear the mandate; they must sweep my way*
> *And marshal me to knavery. Let it work;*
> *For 'tis the sport to have the enginer*
> *Hoist with his own petard; and 't shall go hard*
> *But I will delve one yard below their mines*
> *And blow them at the moon. O, 'tis most sweet*
> *When in one line two crafts directly meet.*

WILLIAM SHAKESPEARE, *Hamlet*, Act 3, Scene 4 (*c.* 1599)

3   Cumulate

VERB

To cumulate is to heap something into a pile, such as a sheaf of papers in an in-tray or a pile of rusting waste at a municipal tip. Accumulate is more commonly used in a variety of contexts but cumulate has its precise uses. Derived from the Latin *cumulare*, meaning 'a burgeoning mass' of some description, the word is also linked meteorologically to cumulus, which describes the density, height and shape of a particular type of cloud – literally, a heap of water vapour.

> *He knew it was slovenly yet he had a tendency to*
> *cumulate his laundry on the bathroom floor and*
> *wash the lot in one go, much to the irritation of his*
> *flatmates.*

4   Farouche

ADJECTIVE

Farouche originates from the Old French word *forasche*,
which was used to describe somebody who lived outside,
such as a wandering vagrant. In English, farouche was
often used, in polite circles, to describe somebody who
was shy or awkward in social situations. An alternative
meaning – less common, but perhaps closer to the original
French – is to use it to describe a person who has become
marginalized or socially excluded on the grounds of their
behaviour, character or lifestyle choices; an outsider.

> *When she first arrived in the country she was
> painfully farouche around groups of people and took
> time to settle in socially.*

5   Handsel

NOUN

A handsel or hansel is an old-fashioned word for a small
gift or tribute given either to children or to workers or
servants. It derives from the Saxon word *handsel*, meaning
'to press or deliver into the hand', and is closely linked
to a Scottish tradition known as 'Auld Hansel Monday',
which fell on the first Monday of the New Year. On this
day, particularly in rural communities, farm workers and
servants were granted a day free from labour and were
visited by their employer who furnished them with a small
gift, often in the form of money, as a thank you for their
service and as an omen of prosperity for the coming year.
Up until the latter half of the nineteenth century, Auld
Hansel Monday was the major winter festival for families,
who would visit each other, break bread together and give

small gifts and good luck charms to children. The custom has been superseded by Christmas and Hogmanay (New Year) in Scotland in modern times, although the date (which changes every year) is still marked on calendars and in diaries. In a general figurative sense, handsel can be used to describe any unexpected windfall that bodes well for the future.

> *'Sir,' said John, as he walked along, 'do you think Mr Laurie will give me a holiday on Handsel Monday?' (the first Monday in the year, and the only holiday the Scottish peasantry ever allow themselves, except, perhaps, in the case of a wedding).*
>
> MARTHA BLACKFORD, *The Eskdale Herd-boy* (1819)

6   Fulcrum

NOUN

The root of the word fulcrum is the Latin verb *fulcire*, which originally meant to prop something up, or provide essential support. Fulcrum then developed into the Latin word for a bedpost. By the middle of the seventeenth century, fulcrum was being used in mechanics to describe the hinge or bracket around which levers operate on machinery. Although the link to mechanics still survives today, fulcrum has developed a figurative meaning and is used to describe the central or pivotal element within a system (or idea/argument).

> *The fulcrum of the CEO's presentation to the board was the need to attract greater foreign investment.*

7 Tchotchke

NOUN

A modern word that entered into English in the 1960s, a tchotchke is an item such as a knick-knack or novelty that has no function or notable worth. The word derives directly from the Yiddish *tshatshke* (which in turn is thought to derive from the old Polish word *czaczko*), basically meaning junk. Classic examples of tchotchkes are holiday souvenirs (fridge magnets, ornamental statuettes, snow domes), commemorative ceramics and anything dubiously deemed 'collectable'. The fact the word is so new suggests the accumulation of largely worthless, functionless jumble is a modern affliction; yard sales and internet auction sites wouldn't exist without tchotchkes.

> *My grandmother was a compulsive hoarder of tchotchkes; every shelf in her house was covered with dust-gathering ornaments and souvenirs acquired on her travels.*

8 Campestral

ADJECTIVE

In Latin, a campus is a field or open space. In ancient Rome, the campus was the space in the city given over to games, gymnastics, military exercises and parades. The adjective campestral relates directly to campus and means 'of or pertaining to a field or wide open space'. As an adjective, the word is used positively to describe the beguiling beauty of natural panoramas, landscapes and views.

> *From the summit of Mount Tai, the campestral views across the valleys and the Shandong tundra are simply breathtaking.*

9 Perspicacious

ADJECTIVE

Perspicacious is often considered to be a synonym of words such as shrewd or astute, and although all three words suggest a sharpness of mind and soundness of judgement, perspicacious evokes a subtle difference. Derived from the Latin verb *perspicere*, meaning 'to examine, observe and see through', perspicacious describes the uncanny ability to see through a problem or situation in order to unearth a hidden solution.

> *Sherlock Holmes had extraordinary perspicacious powers, which enabled him to draw conclusions from seemingly incidental details and random clues.*

10 Nidus

NOUN

Nidus is an interesting example of a word where two related meanings have combined to produce a third figurative meaning, in this case one with darker, negative connotations. *Nidus* is the Latin word for a nest or place of breeding, and nidification is still used today as the scientific term to describe the process of nest building by animals to protect their offspring. In biology and medicine, however, nidus is a term for the locations and conditions where bacteria gather and reproduce. It is therefore from a combination of these scientific meanings where the figurative use of nidus has developed; namely the space where disagreeable ideas, behaviour and actions fester and breed.

> *The nidus of civil unrest was to be found in the ghettos and shanty towns whose inhabitants were ruled over by the drug cartels and suffered at the hands of state corruption.*

11 AND 12 **Cerebral** versus **Cerebrate**

ADJECTIVE/VERB

The term cerebral, in the strictest sense, relates to anything to do with the function or wellbeing of the brain. Derived from the Latin word *cerebrum*, meaning brain, the root word is used specifically in the science of human biology to refer to the large upper part of the brain. The modern adjective cerebral came into usage in English in the early nineteenth century and over time has come to mean almost anything that stimulates the intellect. A rare cousin of cerebral is the verb 'to cerebrate', an elegant way to describe the act of pondering, contemplating or thinking deeply. People of high intellect are often described as cerebral and it could be argued that this has become a slightly lazy use of the adjective – as surely we all have brains and so therefore we are all cerebral.

> *The greatest novels are cerebral and invite readers to think deeply about their subjects.*
>
> *She likes to cerebrate on problems and issues.*

❧

13 AND 14 **Comminute** versus **Triturate**

VERBS

The prefix *com-*, meaning 'with' or 'together', is used in many words in English loaned from Latin and comminute is no exception. The prefix is attached to the Latin verb *minuere*, which means 'to lessen something or cause it to decrease'. Triturate also has its roots in Latin, from the word *triturare*, meaning 'to thresh a substance and reduce it to smaller particles'. Both words share the generalized meaning of something being broken down into constituent parts. One particularly gruesome medical usage of comminute relates specifically to bone fractures. Imagine, if you can without feeling queasy, a shin bone crushed into tiny splinters. Triturate is seldom used, but at a push could describe grinding seeds or spices to create a fine powder.

> *There was relief in the team locker room when news came through that x-rays showed that the running back's fractured leg had not been comminuted.*

> *The key to a good curry paste is to lightly toast the seeds and then triturate them with a pestle and mortar.*

15 AND 16 Magniloquent versus Grandiloquent

ADJECTIVE

Magnus is Latin for 'great' and grandus Latin for 'grand'; combined with *loqui*, 'to speak', and we form the words magniloquent and grandiloquent. Both words are closely related synonyms and there is some dispute amongst lexicographers as to whether there is any notable difference in meaning at all. However, in some recorded usages, a slight difference has been cited and it relates entirely to the attitude of the listening audience. Someone who is a magniloquent speaker is somebody prone to discourse that is wilfully pretentious, pompous, bombastic and probably quite boring and irritating to listen to. Someone who is a grandiloquent speaker has a considerable felicity with words, and although they may use complex, rare and unusual words in their discourse they are used with elegance and style.

Depending entirely on personal opinion, certain politicians are either grandiloquent or magniloquent speakers when addressing parliament.

࿇

17 AND 18 **Bathetic** versus **Pathetic**

ADJECTIVE

Bathos and its sister word pathos sound very similar and as a result are often erroneously used, especially in critical writing on art and literature. Both words have their roots in Greek, *bathos* meaning 'depth' and *pathos* meaning 'suffering or sorrow'.

Around the 1700s, the suffix *-etic* started to be applied in English to the noun apathy to form the adjective apathetic. The same suffix was soon applied to pathos, a word first coined by the philosopher Aristotle in his *Rhetoric* (*circa* fourth century BC), a treatise on the art of persuasion. For Aristotle, pathos was a quality in art, literature and music that elicits or engenders a feeling of sadness. The true and original meaning of the word pathetic is therefore a quality that evokes pity and sorrow – it was only much later, perhaps when the world began to lose a sense of sympathy, that pathetic began to be used informally to describe something or someone weak and inadequate.

Bathos was first coined by the English poet Alexander Pope (1688–1744) in his satirical essay 'Peri Bathous, Or the Art of Sinking in Poetry' (1728). Bathos, for Pope, was an error in judgement by a writer who sinks suddenly from the high ideals of the sublime into crassness, maybe by using a mawkish metaphor or clichéd imagery. Bathetic therefore is the moment when something in art, drama or literature slips suddenly or jars, either intentionally (for comic effect) or otherwise (through misjudgement or ineptitude).

The eulogy was for the main part very moving and heartfelt but had become bathetic by the end when the speaker slipped in a bawdy anecdote about the deceased's toilet habits.

He looked so pathetic shivering in the rain that her heart went out to him.

❦

19   Canker

VERB

In medical terminology, a canker is a sore that spreads across the skin, eating into the tissue. The word originates from the Latin word *cancer* that relates both to a crab (hence also the sign of the zodiac) and to malignant tumours. In English the word cancer mutated into the word canker by the Middle English period and developed a figurative meaning to describe something that has become corrupted by a pernicious influence. Prince Escalus uses the word in Shakespeare's *Romeo and Juliet* to describe the destructive feud between the Capulets and the Montagues:

> *To wield old partisans, in hands as old,*
> *Cankered with peace, to part your cankered hate*

WILLIAM SHAKESPEARE, *Romeo and Juliet*, Act 1, Scene 1 (*c.* 1595)

❦

20 Animadversion

NOUN

The ancient Latin phrase *animum advertere* has the meaning of 'to turn the mind' towards something or someone. *Advertere* is also the root for a number of other words in English, notably advert (something designed to attract the attention of the mind). Just as the mind can turn towards something, it can also naturally turn away or against something or someone, hence adverse also derives from *advertere*. An animadversion is a written or verbal rebuke; in short, adverse criticism.

> *Both clubs received a formal animadversion from the Football Association for failing to control their fans.*

21 Malinger

VERB

The verb 'to malinger' first entered into English in the early nineteenth century. It derives from the French word *malingre*, meaning sickly. In English, however, malingering developed the sense of someone feigning illness, usually to avoid some task or imposed duty. Most people know somebody who suddenly falls ill at a coincidentally convenient time or perhaps you have even phoned in work and pretended to be sick yourself: malingerers and malingering is a modern practice, hence the fact it is a relatively new word in English.

> *Although she had sounded convincing on the phone, she posted photos of herself at the beach on Facebook and was fired for malingering.*

22 Exculpate

VERB

The Latin phrase *mea culpa* is commonly used to acknowledge responsibility for wrongdoing or a mistake and translates as 'my fault'. The Latin word *culpa* means 'blame' and forms the root of several words synonymous with exculpate, subtly differentiated by the degree of seriousness of the accusation or misdemeanour (*see also* culpable, culpatory, disculpate, exonerate, absolve and vindicate). Using the scale of the blame game, someone is exculpated when they are cleared of blame for some minor error, infringement of the rules or deed.

> *When John owned up to eating the last cookies in the jar, Sally felt exculpated from her colleagues' accusations.*

23 Quiddity

NOUN

An unusual word that has several seemingly contrasting meanings through its association with other words. The Latin *quidditas* was used to describe the 'essence' of something or someone, or a clearly defining characteristic (*see also* quintessence). This sense of quiddity dates back in English to the fourteenth century, but over time the word has taken on subsidiary meanings. By the sixteenth century, the quiddity of an argument was the most salient or subtle point (think of the word quibble). By the eighteenth century, a person's quiddities were their quirks or eccentricities, peculiarities that made their character unique.

> *My aunt Jane had many quiddities, one of which was to snort like a pig when she laughed.*

24   Sibilance

NOUN

Sibilance describes an acoustic sound in speech or writing produced by certain consonants when air is pushed from the vocal tracts out of the lips with the tongue pressing against the teeth. The word came into use in the early nineteenth century to describe a particular stylistic device common in poetry that is closely associated with alliteration. The most common sibilant consonant is 's', which produces a hissing sound as in the nursery rhyme 'Sing a Song of Sixpence'. Sibilance is also used as a technical term in linguistics and speech therapy and recently has been applied to digital technology to denote high-frequency hissing on sound recordings.

> *Sweet dreams of pleasant streams*
> *By happy, silent, moony beams*

WILLIAM BLAKE, 'A Cradle Song' (1789)

25   Cerulean

ADJECTIVE

Have you ever gazed up at a cloudless sky and wanted an appropriate adjective to describe it? Well, look no further! Cerulean is a distortion of the Latin word for sky, *caelum*, and *caeruleus*, meaning 'dark blue'. In its strictest sense, cerulean isn't limited to just describing the sky but can be used to describe anything of a deep blue hue such as a crystal clear sea. It is also a popular shade of watercolour paint. Azure is another word often associated with describing the sky, although this word derives not from Latin but from ancient Persian and is thought to have come from lapis lazuli – a semi-precious blue gemstone.

He lay back in the long grass and gazed up at the deep cerulean sky.

⁓

26   Festinate

ADJECTIVE/VERB

William Shakespeare takes credit for the first recorded use of festinate in English in his play *King Lear*. Most likely Shakespeare was drawing upon the Latin *festinatus*, meaning 'to hasten' or 'make haste'. Festinate can be used both as an adjective and a verb and the bard seems to have been rather fond of the word as he also uses it as an adverb in *Love's Labour Lost* (Act 3, Scene 1): 'Bring him festinately hither.' However it is used, it all boils down to doing something with urgency.

> *Advise the Duke where you are going, to a most festinate preparation.*
>
> WILLIAM SHAKESPEARE, *King Lear*, Act 3, Scene 7 (*c.* 1605)

⁓

27   Acolyte

NOUN

The etymology of acolyte is complex, with the word initially entering English from the medieval Latin *acolytus* and Anglo-French *acolit* – a term exclusively used to describe a person assisting the priest during mass. The origins of the term, however, lie in the Greek word *akólouthos,* meaning 'follower', and it is from this definition that the modern use of acolyte has developed over time. An acolyte is a member of a prominent person's entourage and has more than a whiff of fawning sycophancy about it.

> *The Duke made a grand entrance at the ball, closely followed by his train of acolytes and servants.*

❧

28 Halcyon

ADJECTIVE

A word closely linked with feelings of wistful nostalgia. In Greek mythology, Alkyone, the daughter of King Aeolia, is said to have thrown herself into the sea on learning that her husband Ceyx had drowned in a shipwreck. Out of compassion, the gods changed Alkyone into a kingfisher and gave her the ability to build floating nests on the sea, which helped calm the waters. The term 'halcyon days' was used by the Greeks to denote the seven days either side of the winter solstice when the waters were calmed by the gods, so Alkyone could nest-build unhindered by storms. It is from this that the secondary meaning of halcyon developed, to denote a period of calm, tranquillity and prosperity. The word is often used about periods of time seen in hindsight, rather than the present.

> *The 1960s are often viewed as the halcyon days of popular culture.*

❧

29 Mercurial

ADJECTIVE

Another word derived from ancient mythology. The Roman messenger god Mercury was known for his speed and cunning and also his often volatile or changeable temper.

The English adjective mercurial derives directly from the Latin *mercurialis*, which originally meant merely to be born under the sign of Mercury. As belief in matters of astrology developed, and in particular the effect a person's star sign has upon characteristics of their personality, attributes of the god Mercury were applied to people born when the planet was in retrograde. Mercurial in modern usage is used to describe somebody quick-witted and sharp-minded but also unpredictable.

> *John McEnroe was a player of mercurial talents; he frustrated many of his coaches with his inconsistency and unpredictable behaviour on court.*

30 Asseverate

VERB

A rare verb in modern usage but one that entered into English around the 1640s. To asseverate isn't just to make a statement or declaration, but it is to do so with gravitas. The easiest way to remember when to use asseverate is to think of the word 'severe', as both words are linked to the Latin adjective *severus*, meaning serious.

> *When she took to the floor, she asseverated her position with such passion that the usually rowdy chamber was hushed into silence.*

31 Métier

NOUN

A direct borrowing from French which first appeared in English in the eighteenth century. In French, *métier* means simply job or profession but in English it has come to mean a particular skill or occupation to which one is especially suited. In all probability the word slipped into English through aristocratic circles and was, somewhat pretentiously, used by the work-shy and privileged as an elegant excuse for not having a proper job because they were still searching for their métier. Forte is another French borrowing (from *fort*: 'strong'), meaning something at which someone is strong or excels. In English, métier and forte are synonymous.

> *After struggling to find a job after university, she finally found her métier was in public relations.*

32 Ostensible

ADJECTIVE

The Latin verb *ostendere*, meaning 'to show', provides the root for ostensible – but take care when encountering this word as there could be more going on behind the scenes. When somebody provides an 'ostensible' reason for something they are usually drawing attention to surface-level facts, when closer examination may reveal a discrepancy between what has been stated and what is actually the truth.

> *Intelligence reports of hostile activity provided the ostensible reason for the war, although many observers believed there were political and economic motives behind it.*

33 Defenestrate

VERB

To defenestrate someone is commonly used in modern times to describe the sudden removal of a person from a position of prominence or public office. In the strictest sense, however, it means to throw something or someone out of a window. The word derives directly from the Latin word for window, *finestra*, and has the weight of history behind it. On 23 May 1618 in Prague, two imperial regents and their secretary were tried and found guilty of failing to uphold laws protecting religious tolerance and as a result were thrown out of a third-floor window of Prague Castle as punishment. Miraculously, the three men survived the seventy-foot fall, but the incident caused considerable civil unrest and is believed by some historians to be one of the catalysts for the ensuing Thirty Years' War (1618–48) in Central Europe. The episode became known as the Defenestration of Prague and gave rise to the word defenestrate.

> *There had been several failed attempts by her own party to defenestrate the Prime Minister from office, yet somehow she managed to cling on to power.*

34 Fustigate

VERB

Has anyone ever criticized you with such ferocity (justified or otherwise) that you have been left feeling as if you have been beaten around the head? If so, you have been fustigated. In the seventeenth century, the verb 'to fustigate' meant to bash somebody around the head with a cudgel or cosh – or anything that was close to hand and likely to cause damage, for that matter. The word is derived from the Latin noun *fustis*, which was a wooden staff specifically intended to be used for acts of cranial violence. These days, in what is to be hoped less savage times, to fustigate somebody is to severely criticize them verbally.

> *His behaviour at the office Christmas party caused quite a stir and he was soundly fustigated by his boss at work the following day.*

35 Garrulous

ADJECTIVE

The Latin language is loaded with words relating to speech and manners of speaking. One such is *garrire*, which roughly translates as chattering or babbling. A garrulous person could be described as somebody who never knows when to shut up, or is overly enamoured with the sound of their own voice. The content of this constant chattering is usually thought to be of little notable consequence or worth.

> *My mother is very garrulous at family gatherings; she loves nothing better than to hold court at the head of the table and dominate the conversation over dinner.*

36 Cathexis

NOUN

After the medieval period, various faux Latin words filtered into the English language, often by way of scientific terminology or description. Cathexis is such a word (known as New Latin) and first appeared in an academic book on the psychological theories of Sigmund Freud in 1922. Cathexis has its root in the Greek word *kathexis,* which has the meaning of holding or gripping something. In psychoanalysis, cathexis signifies having a strong emotional investment in something or someone, often to detrimental effect. In short, mental obsession.

> *The patient experienced considerable discomfort when he was made to confront his cathexis with his ex-girlfriend.*

⌒⌒⌒

37 Bloviate

VERB

To bloviate is to speak or write in a long-winded and rambling manner. The origins of the word are unclear, although it is often associated with the twenty-ninth President of the United States, Warren G. Harding (in office 1921–23). Harding had a reputation for being overly verbose in his speeches and for using four or five words when one would have sufficed.

> *Sports pundits tend to bloviate in radio commentaries to fill up airtime.*

⌒⌒⌒

38   Maladroit

ADJECTIVE

It is impossible to go through life without encountering somebody so maladroit it drives you to despair. The word is a curious mish-mash of Old and Middle French that entered English in the seventeenth century. The word *mal* meant something bad (as in malign) and *adroit* meant direct or proper, so together it literally means bad direction or improper. The word is most commonly used as a synonym for clumsy and inept, often in relation to other people or socially awkward situations.

> *Uncle John can always be relied upon to make maladroit remarks at family gatherings.*

39   Ineluctable

ADJECTIVE

Wrestling was a major sport in ancient Greece and Rome and was one of the blue ribbon events in the sporting festivals of antiquity, notably the ancient Olympics (Greco-Roman wrestling has featured in every modern Olympics since the Games' inception in 1908). The root of the word ineluctable lies in wrestling; it derives from the Latin word *luctari*, which means 'to wrestle' or, in a figurative sense, 'to struggle'. The adjective ineluctable was then created by adding the negative prefix *in-* to mean something that can't be struggled against, contended or resisted, like trying to escape a paralysing headlock from a brawny Greco-Roman wrestler.

> *The debate around global warming centres on the ineluctable facts surrounding the shrinking polar ice caps.*

`40` , `41` AND `42` **Laudable** versus **Laudatory** versus **Lauded**

ADJECTIVES/VERB

The difference in meaning between laudable, laudatory and lauded is subtle and often they are erroneously used interchangeably. All three words have at their root the Latin verb *laud* meaning 'to praise', but the variation is who or what is receiving the praise. Laudable tends to be used to describe actions that are worthy of praise, despite perhaps being unsuccessful or going unnoticed. Laudatory describes something or someone that has received much positive praise, as in laudatory reviews of books or films. And finally, lauded relates to having received praise for an action.

> *He made a laudable suggestion in order to reach a compromise.*

> *The court poet composed many laudatory verses in the king's honour.*

> *He was lauded for his efforts in reaching a compromise.*

`43` **Rectitude**

NOUN

In Latin, *rectus* can mean both 'right' and 'straight'. In medical terminology, therefore, rectus refers to straight or parallel muscles such as the *rectus abdominis* muscles commonly known as 'abs', definition of which is highly prized by gym fanatics. Rectitude relates to moral straightness or righteousness; to be unwavering in one's beliefs or ideas.

A sense of moral rectitude was behind his decision to resign from the board of directors.

❧

44 Lugubrious

ADJECTIVE

A lovely word – say it out loud, nice and slowly, lu-gu-bri-ous; it has a sonorous quality that reflects its sorrowful aspect. The Latin verb *lugēre,* meaning 'to mourn', provides the basis for lugubrious, which describes anything forlorn, gloomy or sad. Lugubrious once had a sibling English word in luctual, an elegant adjective that specifically meant something that was mournful or provoked mournful emotions. Sadly, luctual has long since become obsolete, leaving lugubrious all alone in the world to mourn its passing. Lugubrious is often used negatively to describe something (or someone) that is excessively downbeat or depressing.

> *She found his lugubrious personality could really bring her down after any concentrated period of time in his company.*

❧

45 Sanguine

ADJECTIVE/NOUN

In medieval medicine, to have a sanguine complexion was a positive thing; it meant to have blood in the cheeks and was a sign of good health. Sanguine derives from the Latin word for blood, *sanguis*, which also provides the root for several other words such as sanguineous (containing or related to blood) and sanguinolent (tinged with or containing traces of blood). When used as a noun, albeit rarely, sanguine is the colour of blood, but it is to the medieval medical definition that the adjective defers in its modern sense: that of maintaining a rosy and optimistic outlook.

> *The manager maintained a sanguine attitude about his team's chances during the television interviews, despite missing several key players due to injury.*

❧

46 Panegyric

NOUN

In ancient Greece it was common on certain days of the year for towns and cities to hold public meetings called *panēgyreis* (meaning 'an assembly for all'). At these meetings, speakers would address the audience with rousing speeches, extolling the great achievements of the cities and their leaders, rather in the fashion of modern political rallies. The word was borrowed into English in the seventeenth century and has come to describe a rousing speech or piece of writing that eulogizes or praises someone or something.

> *The newspapers contained many panegyrics in honour of the anniversary of Shakespeare's birth.*

❧

47 Recuse

VERB

The current meaning of recuse relates to legal terminology and came into common usage in the mid-twentieth century. To recuse oneself from a trial or public investigation is to remove oneself from the position of being in judgement, usually due to a conflict of interest. The word, however, has existed in English, albeit with different meanings, since the fourteenth century. Deriving from the Anglo-French word *recuser*, it originally had the meaning of 'to refuse or reject'. Later on, in the seventeenth century, the word started to be used in legal jargon to mean challenging or rejecting the verdict of a judge or magistrate. Judges at some point decided to reclaim the word for themselves if they had to disqualify themselves from a trial or inquest.

> *The President was reported to have been enraged when his attorney general recused himself from the investigation.*

---

48 Spavined

ADJECTIVE

In Shakespeare's *The Taming of the Shrew*, Petruchio turns up deliberately late to his wedding, dressed in mismatched and shambolic clothes and riding the most decrepit horse he could possibly find. This is all part of Petruchio's plan to 'tame' Catherine by humiliating her on their wedding day and to this end he has chosen to ride a spavined horse. The term 'spavins' relates to bony growths on a horse's leg joints or hocks that cause severe lameness. A spavined horse was one well past its sell-by date and over time the term spavined came to be applied to anything that was over the hill or nearly obsolete. Below is part of Biondello's colourful description of Petruchio's poor, diseased horse:

> *His horse hipped – with an old mothy saddle and stirrups of no kindred – besides, possessed with the glanders and like to mose in the chine, troubled with the lampass, infected with the fashions, full of*

> *windgalls, sped with spavins, rayed with the yellows,*
> *past cure of the fives, stark spoiled with the staggers,*
> *begnawn with the bots, swayed in the back and*
> *shoulder-shotten, [...]*

WILLIAM SHAKESPEARE, *The Taming of the Shrew*,
Act 3, Scene 2 (*c.* 1590)

❧

49 Mansuetude

NOUN

The Latin verb *mansuescere* means to tame something,
usually a horse. It was formed by *manus*, meaning 'hand',
and *suescere*, 'to accustom' – being brought to hand,
in other words. The rare English noun mansuetude
describes qualities of tameness and/or a meek and gentle
disposition.

> *My cat exudes mansuetude, as she is mild-mannered*
> *and very affectionate.*

❧

50 Nebulous

ADJECTIVE

When something is said to be nebulous it is because it is
indistinct or vague. In Latin, *nebulosus* is something misty
or foggy and which hinders clarity. The word nebula also
came to be applied to the cosmos and let's face it, there
isn't anything more elusive than distant galaxies and
nebulae.

> *He persisted in giving nebulous replies when*
> *questioned about his party's policies.*

51 Diaphanous

ADJECTIVE

The Greek verb *diaphainein*, meaning 'to show through', forms the root for diaphanous – a word commonly used to describe fine, willowy fabrics that are almost see-through but not quite transparent. It is this delicacy of form that leads art critics to describe wispy, ethereal landscape paintings as diaphanous. A less common use of the word is to describe anything that is slightly vague or lacking substance – such as a diaphanous argument or reason.

> *The actress caused quite a stir at the Academy Awards by wearing a low-cut diaphanous frock.*

52 Contrite

ADJECTIVE

To be contrite describes feeling bad about one's actions; being apologetic, sorry or remorseful. Contrite entered the English language via Anglo-French from the Latin verb *conterere*, meaning 'to bruise' or 'to grind'. Hence, a person who is contrite feels that way because they have bruised another's feelings. *Conterere* itself was formed by combining the prefix *con-* and *terere*, meaning 'to rub'; therefore the contrite person has rubbed someone the wrong way.

> *She felt contrite over her hastiness in condemning her friend without checking her facts first.*

53 Extenuate

VERB

To extenuate means to attempt to lessen the seriousness of something by glossing over or excusing an act or behaviour. It is commonly used in the phrase 'extenuating circumstances', whereby a reason is sought to explain away the significance of something. Extenuate was derived in the sixteenth century from the Latin word *extenuatus*, the past participle of the verb *extenuare*, meaning 'to make thin' or 'to make light of'.

> *He tried to extenuate his son's bad behaviour in letting down his neighbour's tyres by insisting that it was just a childish prank.*

54 Anthropomorphic

ADJECTIVE

Anthropomorphic describes non-human objects that are given human characteristics, for example ascribing human traits to animals in children's stories. The word derives from the late Latin word *anthrōpomorphus*, which itself comes from the Greek *anthrōpos* meaning 'human being', and *morphē*, or form.

> *All the anthropomorphic characters in the Winnie-the-Pooh books all have distinctive human traits. We all know an Eeyore!*

55 Retrodict

VERB

First used in the 1950s, retrodict was formed from 'retro' and 'predict' to create a word for predicting the past, retro meaning backwards. Predict has been used in English since the early seventeenth century as meaning 'to envisage or foresee future happenings', formed by joining the Latin words *prae* (meaning 'before') and *dīcere* (meaning 'to say').

> *It was possible to retrodict what had happened at the burial site by studying the ancient artefacts found nearby.*

56 Refection

NOUN

Refection is one of the numerous words in the English language for food or nourishment, but it can also be used to describe a way of restoring one's physical, mental or spiritual sustenance. Originally *refeccioun* in Middle English, it was borrowed from the Anglo-French *refectiun*, which itself comes from Latin *refectio*, meaning 'refreshment' or 'repairing'.

> *After a long day hiking, the group all looked forward to the refection provided at the hostel along with a good night's sleep.*

57 Vapid

ADJECTIVE

Signifying a lack of spirit or character, vapid first entered the English language during the seventeenth century. It's derived from the Latin *vapidus*, meaning 'flat-tasting'; it is still used in this sense by wine connoisseurs. The word can also be applied as a derogatory term to describe a person or a situation that is flat, insipid or inane.

> *Veronica, who always likes to hold court at dinner parties, tells the same old vapid stories we've all heard before.*

58 AND 59 Stanch versus Staunch

VERBS

The verb stanch and the variant staunch stem from the Anglo-French word *estancher* (which has the same meaning as stanch), and have both been used in English for centuries. They both mean to stop the flow of something but staunch is more commonly used as an adjective to describe loyalty – for example, someone being a staunch friend – whereas stanch is normally used only as a verb, e.g to stanch the flow of blood. They are technically interchangeable; however, some wordsmiths advise keeping them apart and this sentence can help with their usage: 'A *staunch* supporter campaigning on behalf of the party could *stanch* the flow of votes going to the opposition.' Alternatively, this old limerick can help in defining their usage:

> *Tho' neither stanch nor staunch must conform*
> *To rigid semantical norm*
> *Some editors will blanch,*

When encountering stanch
If it's used in adjective form.

❧

60   **Maudlin**

ADJECTIVE

First recorded in the English language in 1509, maudlin is used to describe someone being emotional or tearful (often with reference to being drunk) and derives from the Biblical image of Mary Magdalene as a weeping and penitent sinner, washing Christ's feet with her tears. Maudlin can, therefore, be used to describe a tearful drunk or someone who is seemingly over-emotional and regretful.

> *After her fourth glass of wine, Linda became a*
> *maudlin wreck, weeping uncontrollably on her*
> *friend's shoulder and saying she wished she'd never*
> *asked her husband to leave.*

❧

61   **Anachronism**

NOUN

The noun anachronism was first used in the English language in the seventeenth century with reference to an error in the dating of something but, nowadays, it also refers to something that is out of place chronologically or in terms of time. It stems from the Greek words *chronos* meaning 'time' and the prefix *ana-*, meaning 'up', 'back' or 'again'.

> *In his quest for self-sufficiency, John was an*
> *anachronism in the modern world, refusing to*
> *comply with societal norms, living in a handmade*
> *tent and foraging for food.*

62 Otiose

ADJECTIVE

The first recorded use of otiose was in 1795 as a term to mean something that produces no useful outcome or result. However, by the nineteenth century it was being used to mean idle, from its Latin stem *otiosus* meaning 'at leisure'. Otiose can be used to describe anything superficial and lacking substance. The noun form *otiosity*, which is seldom used today, predates *otiose* by around three hundred years.

> *The examiner gave Peter's essay very low marks and commented that a large part of it was otiose rambling.*

63 Opprobrium

NOUN

Opprobrium refers to public disgrace or blame. The word was borrowed from Latin in the seventeenth century and comes from the verb *opprobrare*, meaning 'to reproach'. The adjective opprobrious also comes from this source, meaning 'infamous' or 'scurrilous'.

> *The unscrupulous landlord, who charged high rents for almost uninhabitable properties, was met with opprobrium by the public when he was exposed in a documentary.*

64   Recalcitrant

ADJECTIVE

If someone is recalcitrant it means they are stubborn or defiant but it can also be used to describe a mechanism or system that is difficult to operate, as well as something which is not responsive to treatment such as an illness or disease. The term was first used in English during the 1840s to describe a human behaviour, but the ancient Romans used *recalcitrare* initially to describe stubborn horses or mules (as the word literally means 'kick back') and later humans who bore this trait and kicked back against authority.

> *The recalcitrant youth was sentenced to a further six months in prison due to his refusal to abide by the rules of the institution.*

65 and 66   Timorous versus Timid

ADJECTIVES

Timorous describes someone who is fearful, as does the adjective timid. Both derive from the Latin verb *timēre*, meaning 'to fear', but timorous came into use in the English language during the mid-fifteenth century, whereas timid was coined around a hundred years later. As well as describing a human or animal who is easily frightened, both can be used to illustrate a gesture or movement indicating fear.

> *The little boy gave the teacher a timorous smile when he was introduced to her on his first day at school.*
>
> *The kitten was very timid around humans.*

67 Vituperative

ADJECTIVE

The first known use of this adjective in the English language was in 1727, and it is defined as 'containing criticism, disapproval or condemnation' – in other words, it's a way of describing verbal abuse.

> *She closed down her Facebook account as she could no longer stand the unwarranted vituperative comments she was receiving.*

68 Unctuous

ADJECTIVE

Nowadays, unctuous is used to describe someone who is fake, two-faced or insincere, and can also be employed as a term to describe something that is fatty or oily in texture or appearance. Originally, when the term came into the English language during the fourteenth century, it was not derogatory but instead referred to the act of healing, as it derived from the Latin verb *ungere* ('to anoint'), which also gave us the word ointment. However, the connotation could have come about due to the idea that someone who is insincere is also oily or smarmy.

> *Having met Jimmy through an internet dating site, she quickly came to the conclusion that he was an unctuous individual who wasn't revealing his true character.*

69   Cachinnate

VERB

A relatively new word that first appeared in English in written form in the early nineteenth century, the verb 'to cachinnate' means to laugh loudly and immodestly – a real full-on belly laugh. The Latin word *cachinnare* has the same meaning and is thought to have been coined to describe the sound of loud, intrusive laughter, giving the word an onomatopoeic quality.

> *The audience cachinnated at the comedian's act until their sides ached.*

70   Vindicate

VERB

The original Latin root for vindicate is *vindicatus*, which has the meaning of setting something free or avenging a wrongdoing. This meaning is more or less becoming obsolete but vindicate retains a sense of restorative justice in its present form. A person is vindicated when their actions are proved to be correct despite having been questioned or criticized in the past.

> *The coach's decision to play the young striker from the start was fully vindicated by a match-winning performance from the rookie.*

71 **Exonerate**

VERB

When we place an onus on something we weight it down with a burden or expectation. In the sixteenth century, to exonerate something was to unburden it and it was used to describe, for example, unloading a ship's cargo. Over time, this unburdening took on a legal meaning 'to free: from charges or accusations'.

> *The police force claimed the report completely exonerated their officers from blame.*

⁓

72 **Culpable**

ADJECTIVE

In Latin, *culpare* means 'to blame' and *culpa* is 'fault'. When somebody is culpable of something they are guilty and deserving of blame. There is a subtle implication, however, that although a culpable person is deserving of blame they may have escaped sanction or censure. It also carries the sense that they aren't necessarily guilty in the sense of deliberate wrongdoing but instead have perhaps committed an error of judgement or oversight.

> *The company denied they were culpable for the accident and claimed stringent safety procedures had been followed.*

⁓

73 Capricious

ADJECTIVE

The English noun caprice means something characterized by instability or unpredictability and it is from this word that the adjective capricious is formed. Caprice originally had the meaning 'of a whim' although its roots are somewhat more sinister. The word derives from the Italian word *capriccio*, which had the original meaning 'of a shudder' or 'shiver of fear'. *Capo* in Italian means head and *riccio* is the word for hedgehog. This in turn led to a figurative use of capriccio to describe a sudden hair-raising experience as akin to having a hedgehog on one's head. A capricious person in English, however, isn't somebody in shock, but a person prone to suddenly changing their mind or doing something on a whim.

> *Her capricious boss was prone to making sudden sweeping decisions without the prior consultation of the rest of the team.*

74 Putative

ADJECTIVE

The Latin verb *putare* means 'to consider' or 'to think' and hence anything putative is considered to be or assumed to be so, as opposed to something definitely known. In everyday usage, putative is positioned before the object in a sentence and acts as a modifier. Therefore, it is correct to say there were putative reasons behind a course of action, but incorrect to say the reasons were putative.

> *The coroner adjudged that suicide was the putative cause of death.*

75 Voluble

ADJECTIVE

In Latin, *volubilis* is used to describe something that is rolling or twisting. A voluble person is someone for whom words seem to roll off the tongue with graceful speed. The word differs from close synonyms such as loquacious or garrulous in that it is usually used in a slightly more positive sense. A voluble person is someone who might be worth listening to, whereas a garrulous person most likely isn't.

> *I met a very voluble chap on the train who told me several amusing anecdotes about his days in the armed forces.*

76 Malediction

NOUN

From the fourteenth century onwards, if you heaped maledictions upon someone it meant you were speaking ill of them. In Latin, *maledicere* means to speak evil or to place a curse upon someone, with the word *mal* (bad) also providing the root for related words such as malign and malignant.

> *I taunted him, ridiculed him, loaded him with maledictions, though the saints know they were uttered in the idle peevishness of impatience.*
>
> SIR WALTER SCOTT, *The Fair Maid of Perth* (1828)

77 AND 78 **Incipient** versus **Insipid**

ADJECTIVES

Everything has to start somewhere and so it is with incipient. The word is derived from the Latin verb *incipere*, meaning 'to begin'. Incipient first entered into English via scientific texts in the seventeenth century (incipient theories) and specifically in medicine to describe newly discovered diseases or treatments. The word should not be confused with insipid, which describes something weak.

> *Medical research continues to develop incipient treatments for cancer.*

> *The meal was a big disappointment; even the soup was cold and insipid.*

79 **Obdurate**

ADJECTIVE

In Latin, the adjective *durus* is used to describe something hard or strong and is the root for the word durable. Obdurate is not always a positive adjective, however, as an obdurate person is usually stubborn and difficult to persuade once their mind is made up.

> *He was an obdurate smoker and blatantly ignored the advice of his doctors by refusing to attempt to give up.*

80 Canorous

ADJECTIVE

A pleasant-sounding adjective, which is just as well as that is exactly what it means. Derived from the Latin verb *canere*, meaning 'to sing', a canorous sound is agreeable to the ear. Other related words from the same root included cantor, the lead voice in a choir (and so presumably the best singer) and canto – the Italian word for song which is also a section of an epic poem.

> *He sang out a long, loud, and canorous peal of laughter, that might have wakened the Seven Sleepers.*
>
> THOMAS DE QUINCEY, *The Confessions of an English Opium Eater* (1821)

81 Enervate

ADJECTIVE

A word that is often mistaken in meaning as it is similar sounding to elevate and energize. To become enervated isn't to become in any way rejuvenated or refreshed, though; quite the opposite, in fact. *Nervus* in Latin can mean either sinew or nerves and the word relates to physical deterioration, mental tiredness or general apathy. There is a subsidiary use of the word to describe a lengthy process of weakening almost to the point of inertia.

> *The stress of his job had left him enervated and stifled his ambitions.*

82 Vitiate

VERB

The Latin noun *vitium* means 'vice' or 'fault' and so to vitiate is to make something defective or corrupted. The word differs from pervert, which has the sense of twisting something away from its natural form. Something is vitiated when faults or errors are allowed to disturb the purity or effectiveness of something.

> *The election was vitiated by lies, scaremongering and misinformation on both sides of the political divide.*

83 Zibeline

NOUN/ADJECTIVE

Zibeline, strictly speaking, is a type of soft, lush fabric woven from camel or alpaca hair. The word originates from Slavic languages where it was the name for a sable, a small mammal of the weasel family. The word has recently developed an adjectival usage to describe anything that is soft and lustrous to touch.

> *Her Persian cat had zibeline-like fur that she found soothing to stroke.*

84   Perforce

ADVERB

A subtle and elegant word, perforce came into English via Anglo-French in the fourteenth century. It is basically a distortion of the French *par*, meaning 'by' and force, which has the same meaning in English and French. Perforce originally meant simply to action something by physical coercion but over time it developed a secondary sense, still prevalent today, defined as 'by the force of circumstance or out of necessity'. Interestingly, Shakespeare uses the word in both senses in two different plays; maybe he was just showing off his felicity with language.

> *He rush'd into my house and took perforce my ring away: this course I fittest choose; for forty ducats is too much to lose*

WILLIAM SHAKESPEARE, *The Comedy of Errors*, Act 4, Scene 3 (*c.* 1594)

> *The lives of all your loving complices*
> *Lean on your health, the which, if you give o'er*
> *To stormy passion, must perforce decay.*

WILLIAM SHAKESPEARE, *Henry IV Part Two*, Act 1, Scene 1 (*c.* 1597)

85 AND 86   Susurrus versus Susurration

NOUNS

It's a secret so whisper it quietly, but it took almost five hundred years for the noun susurration (first used *c.* 1400) to turn into its synonym susurrus in the late eighteenth century, although both words are still in use today.

A susurration or susurrus is any sound that resembled a whisper or a murmur and they derive from the Latin noun *susurrus*. Quite why it took so long for the original form of the word to reassert itself is anyone's guess; perhaps all that whispering and murmuring meant nobody was really listening. The words are often used figuratively and poetically to describe natural sounds like the rustling of leaves in the wind or the bubbling of a brook or stream.

> *From their rented villa they could hear the susurrus of the lapping of the tide upon the shingle down below in the cove.*

> *The principal left the stage to the sound of the pupils' sussuration.*

∽

87   Fugacious

ADJECTIVE

It is the fleeting moments in life – the chance encounters, the happy accidents and joyful coincidences – that one should savour because they fade so soon. That is what the word fugacious is all about: the here today and gone tomorrow. Derived from the Latin verb *fugere*, meaning 'to flee' (usually from a battle scene or fight), fugacious is often used in botany to describe plants and flowers with a short blooming period. Used figuratively it describes any experience or moment that is bright and joyful but sadly over all too soon.

> *Those brief, fugacious times we spent together are burned into my most treasured memories.*

∽

88 Gloaming

NOUN

Gloaming is all about the quality of light, that unique moment between night and day called the twilight. The national anthem of the United States of America actually has a dreadful solecism in its second line: 'Oh, say! can you see by the dawn's early light / What so proudly we hailed at the twilight's last gleaming?' It should of course be gloaming, not gleaming, as only things that reflect light and shine can be said to be gleaming. Twilight, by contrast, has light diminishing by the moment, creating a half-light known, particularly in Scotland, as the gloaming. The word derives from the Old English word for dusk: *glōm*.

> *The lovers met by the old oak tree in the gloaming, knowing they would not be seen.*

89 Peripeteia

NOUN

Aristotle used the word peripeteia when writing his treatise on classical Greek tragedy, *Poetics*, referring to the moment in a play when the protagonist's fortunes shift suddenly from good to bad. The word derives from the Greek verb *peripiptein*, meaning 'to suddenly change or fall down'. It is largely a word used by literary critics and writers but can be used for real situations – a sudden fall from grace by a once prominent and respected person can be described as peripeteia.

> *After his unexpected Olympic success, the sprinter suffered a public peripeteia when the doping rumours started to circulate.*

90 Weltschmerz

NOUN

One of a handful of German words borrowed directly into English, weltschmerz entered into the language in the mid-nineteenth century. The word was first coined by the German novelist Jean Paul in his novel *Selina* (1827). The word is formed by combining the German words for world (*welt*) and pain (*schmerz*) and reflects a deep feeling of melancholy that the state of the world is not what it should be when measured against ideals of human existence.

> *He had given up listening to news programmes on the radio in the mornings as he found it filled him with a gloomy sense of weltschmerz.*

91 Erroneous

ADJECTIVE

The original sense of erroneous derived from the Latin *errare*, which meant 'to wander'. In a figurative sense, something erroneous strays from the path of truth and correctness and is used to describe something that contains errors or mistakes. Erroneous is often used in conjunction with ideas or concepts, such as erroneous notions or arguments.

> *Many people retain the erroneous belief that the words 'that' and 'which' are interchangeable.*

92   Tenebrous

ADJECTIVE

The Latin word for darkness is *tenebrae* and forms the root for the adjective tenebrous. It is a shadowy word, steeped in gloom and murkiness and is used to describe an absence of clear light or, in a figurative sense, anything that is shrouded in darkness or obscurity. The Italian painter Carravaggio (1571–1610) is credited with creating a style of Baroque painting known as tenebrism in which figures lurk in shadows and there are dramatic contrasts between light and dark.

> *She purchased a light box to help with the depression that afflicted her during the tenebrous days of deep midwinter.*

93   Saturnine

ADJECTIVE

As with mercurial and Mercury, ancient Romans believed that people born when the planet Saturn was rising had personality traits inherited from their birth sign. Saturn was the Roman god of agriculture and was often depicted as a stooped, stubborn and dour old man. Someone with a saturnine temperament, therefore, is a person prone to bouts of sullenness and cynicism, who is sardonic and pessimistic in outlook.

> *Her suggestion was met with his usual saturnine smile.*

94   Cimmerian

ADJECTIVE

The Cimmerians were thought to be an ancient nomadic tribe of Indo-Europeans centred around the north Caucasus and the Black Sea in the eighth and ninth century BC. It is from Homer that the meaning of the word Cimmerian derives, however, as archaeological evidence of the lost tribe is inconclusive. In the *Odyssey*, Homer describes a race of people named the *Kimmerioi* who live in a land of mist and darkness at the edge of the world by the entrance to Hades. As a result, anything described as Cimmerian is very dark and gloomy.

> *Where brooding Darkness spreads his jealous wings,*
> *And the night-raven sings;*
> > *There under ebon shades, and low-brow'd rocks,*
> *As ragged as thy locks,*
> *In dark Cimmerian desert ever dwell.*

JOHN MILTON, 'L'Allegro' (1645)

~~~

95   Pungle

VERB

A curious word that appears to have entered into American English from Spanish. To pungle is to pay money and derives from *póngale* in Spanish, meaning 'to put something down'. It seems likely that the word developed from the convention of placing money on gaming tables in games of chance – to pungle down was to double the amount of money staked. Pungle is often used with the prepositions 'up' and 'down' – to pungle up is to pay someone money owed. Mark Twain uses the word in his classic novel *The Adventures of Huckleberry Finn* in a scene when Pap Finn, Huck's abusive, alcoholic father, attempts to get his hands on Huck's fortune.

> 'I hain't got no money, I tell you. You ask Judge Thatcher; he'll tell you the same.'

> 'All right. I'll ask him; and I'll make him pungle, too, or I'll know the reason why. Say, how much you got in your pocket? I want it.'

MARK TWAIN, *The Adventures of Huckleberry Finn* (1884)

---

96   Palimpsest

NOUN

In ancient times, parchments for writing on were in short supply and so often documents were recycled and written over. The Greek word *palimpsēstos* means 'to scrape again' and reflects this practice of scratching writing on top of other writing. The modern sense of a palimpsest is anything that has many layers placed on top of each other.

> *Venice is an architectural palimpsest with buildings from different eras built in layers.*

---

97   Countermand

VERB

The Latin verb *mandare* means 'to entrust' or 'to order' and it is from this word that mandate also derives. To countermand is to reverse or revoke a previous order or command or place an order contrary to a previous command. The word has existed in English since the fourteenth century.

> *The officer chose to countermand the orders of his superiors as he thought he'd be sending his men to certain death.*

~~~

98   Ephemeral

ADJECTIVE

The Greek word *ephēmeros* means 'lasting a day'; its English equivalent ephemeral was originally a medical term for short-lived fevers and ailments. The term also entered into botany to describe plants, flowers and organisms with fleeting blooming periods or lifespans. Recently, the word has come to be used to describe anything transient or here today but gone tomorrow.

> *The pleasures of a holiday are ephemeral but memories linger on.*

~~~

99   Hypermnesia

NOUN

If amnesia is sudden loss of memory, usually as a result of brain trauma, it makes sense that there must be an opposite condition. There is and it is known as hypermnesia – a psychological condition in which patients experience vivid, almost complete, memory recall often either due to trauma or via hypnosis.

> *Mnemonists or 'memory men' were popular in music hall entertainment, wowing audiences with astounding powers of hypermnesia.*

100 Asperity

NOUN

The Latin word *asper* means 'rough' and provides the root for exasperate – a terse and coarse emotional response. Asperity also derives from the same source and the word asper, although rare, also exists in English as an adjective for harsh or severe. If somebody reacts with asperity they are usually angry or bitter, stern and intense.

> *Whether the probability of escaping from the consequences of this ill-timed discovery was delightful to the spinster's feelings, or whether the hearing herself described as a 'lovely woman' softened the asperity of her grief, we know not. She blushed slightly, and cast a grateful look on Mr Jingle.*

CHARLES DICKENS, *The Pickwick Papers* (1836)

101 Inexorable

ADJECTIVE

The Latin root of inexorable is *inexorabilis*, which is formed by the negative prefix *in-* ('not') and *exorabilis*, meaning 'compliance'. Originally, the word had this sense of something or someone that couldn't be shifted or wouldn't be moved by any amount of entreaty, hence immovable. The meaning has slightly changed since it came into English in the fifteenth century and in modern usage it is usually applied to situations that are relentless and cannot be arrested.

> *The inexorable decline of the attention spans of young people has been blamed on modern technology.*

102 Supine

ADJECTIVE

Supine describes somebody lying face upwards on their back and derives from Middle English *suppyne* (first used during the fifteenth century), which itself comes from the Latin *supinus*, similar to the Latin for *sub*, meaning 'under' or 'up to'. If a person is lying in a supine position this suggests laziness, inactivity or apathy.

> *Tom derided his teenage son's habit of lying supine on the sofa for what seemed to be hours on end.*

103 Rubescent

ADJECTIVE

First used in English in *circa* 1731 and deriving from the Latin *rubere* ('to be red'), rubescent describes something reddening or flushing.

> *It was clear from her rubescent cheeks that she was embarrassed by his unkind remarks.*

104 Renitent

ADJECTIVE

Deriving from the Latin *reniti* ('to resist'), renitent was first recorded as being used in English in 1604 and means resisting physical pressure.

> *The protester put up a renitent struggle when the policemen tried to arrest him.*

105 Sequacious

ADJECTIVE

Sequacious is an uncomplimentary term to describe someone who is happy to adopt an idea or opinion without giving it much thought. Derived from the Latin *sequac* or *sequax*, meaning 'inclined to follow', the first recorded use of the word in English was 1643.

> *Harry's sequacious personality was clearly demonstrated when he joined a political party simply in order to ingratiate himself with his new employer.*

106 Pontificate

VERB

To pontificate is to express a view in a pretentious or inflexible manner. It can also mean to preside as a pontiff or pope. In ancient Rome, prior to Christianity, pontifices were powerful priests who controlled the civil law relating to interactions with those gods recognized by the state. The word derives from the Latin *pons* ('bridge') and *facere* ('to make') and it is alleged that pontifices were associated with the sacred bridge over the River Tiber, which could be the connection. Initially, in the fifteenth century, pontificate was used in English to denote things associated with the Pope or priests but, by the early eighteenth century, it was also being used to refer, irreverently, to someone speaking in a ridiculously authoritative manner.

> *She had just spent half an hour pontificating to her friends about the correct way to train a dog.*

107 Seditious

ADJECTIVE

First used in fifteenth-century English, seditious is used to describe the behaviour of individuals or groups who provoke or take part in the act of sedition – that is, rebelling or rising up against lawful authority.

> *The jailed protesters were branded as seditious by the popular press.*

108 Moribund

ADJECTIVE

The literal meaning of the adjective moribund is 'approaching death', deriving from the Latin *moribundus*, which itself is rooted in *mori* ('to die') and entered the English language in the early seventeenth century. However, it is now commonly used to describe something that is obsolete or inactive. Moribund is also sometimes used figuratively to describe something so dull and stultifying that death would be a welcome release.

> *The moribund video player was gathering dust on the shelf under the stairs.*

109 Harbinger

NOUN

Deriving from the Anglo-French word *herberge*, meaning 'lodgings', from as far back as the twelfth century harbinger was the name given to someone providing a place to stay. By the fourteenth century, the definition had changed to mean someone who was sent ahead of a group to find accommodation, but both these meanings have now ceased to be used in English. Since the mid-fifteenth century, harbinger has come to mean a person or thing that helps to introduce change, or a pioneering activity, method or technology. It is also used to refer to something that heralds a future happening or sign that something is about to happen.

> *The invention of the steam engine was the harbinger of the industrial revolution.*

110 Servitude

NOUN

Servitude is another word for slavery, whereby a person or people are not at liberty to act on their own free will and are controlled or 'owned' by others. The word is rooted in the Anglo-French *servitute* from the Latin *servitudo* ('slavery'), and was used in the English language from the fifteenth century. A less common usage for the word describes a right by which someone can stipulate a specific use for something owned by another – for example, a plot of land.

> *African men, women and children who had been captured by rival tribes were sold to traders and shipped off, in appalling conditions, to live a life of servitude in the New World.*

111   Carouse

VERB

A carouse is an excessive drinking session, the word entering the English language in the mid-fifteenth century, being picked up originally from German (*gar aus* meaning 'all out'), via French (*boire carous*: 'to drink all out'). Revellers would toast each other's health and drink their mug of spirits straight down to the bottom, drinking it 'all out'. A carouse not only became a name for a drinking bout but also to take part in a carouse implied participating in debauched behaviour.

> *Fred's stag night was a lively carouse which led to many hangovers the following day.*

112   Ersatz

ADJECTIVE

Ersatz is the German word for 'substitute'. The word first entered into English during the First World War when in the trenches certain commodities in short supply were substituted for other substances. Over time, the word has developed into a general term for anything that is artificial or a poor substitute for the original.

> *The ersatz cover versions of classic songs by contestants on television talent shows are hardly a yardstick of genuine talent.*

113 **Abstemious**

ADJECTIVE

The words abstemious and abstain are often thought
to be synonymous but in fact they derive from different
Latin roots. To be abstemious is to deny oneself the joys
of intoxicating drinks, as the Latin root noun *tēmētum*
basically means booze. The Middle English/Anglo-French
word *abstinēre*, however, means 'to hold back from
or refrain'. One can abstain from anything but only an
abstemious person refuses a drink.

Many people like to play at being abstemious,
especially in January after weeks of self-indulgence.

114 **Hyperbole**

NOUN

Originally, hyperbole was a technical term in the study
of rhetoric but over time it has come into modern usage.
A commonly mispronounced word, hyperbole derived
from the Greek word *hyperbolē*, meaning 'to exceed'.
The addition of the macron (a small slash above the ē)
denotes that the word should be pronounced with a long
vowel sound at the end. Hyperbole is deliberate and often
extravagant use of exaggeration in speech or written
language, often used for persuasive effect.

Mrs Jones was known for being somewhat prone
to hyperbole when it came to gushing about her
daughter's many supposed talents.

115 Neophyte

NOUN

The Latin word *neophytus* originally meant newly planted. The term neophyte initially related to the Catholic Church and novice monks were known as neophytes. This led in turn to the word becoming generally used to mean a recent convert to a religion or faith and, by extension, someone new or unaccustomed to something.

> *I'm a total neophyte with computers; I can only just about turn them on.*

116 Pachydermatous

ADJECTIVE

Pachydermatous, meaning thick-skinned, is derived from Greek and was adopted by the French zoologist, Georges Cuvier, in the late 1700s to classify thick-skinned, hoofed mammals such as elephants, rhinoceroses and hippopotamuses (*pachydermata*). The word can also be used in the metaphorical sense to describe a callous, insensitive person.

> *A pachydermatous person feels nothing for the rough sleeper in the doorway.*

117 Effulgent

ADJECTIVE

Anything that shines with splendour and brilliance can be described as effulgent. To effulge is to shine forth, although as a verb, effulge has never quite taken off. Both words have their root in one of the many Latin words for shine, *fulgēre*.

> *As if from the heavens, an effulgent light shone down through the parted clouds.*

❧

118 Ergophobia

NOUN

Although in Latin *ergo* means 'therefore', in Greek it is the word for work. Ergophobia is therefore a fear of work, something most right-minded people will surely experience at some point in their life.

> *I haven't applied for a job for years as I suffer from ergophobia.*

❧

119 AND 120 Whereof versus Whereon

RELATIVE ADVERBS

Two easily confused relative adverbs. Whereof means the subject that I wish to speak of, i.e. 'of what' or 'of which'. Whereon means 'on which', in terms of physical location.

> *Whereof one cannot speak, thereof one must be silent.*
>
> LUDWIG WITTGENSTEIN, *Tractatus Logico-Philosophicus* (1922)
>
> *To visit the temples of Egypt is to glimpse the foundations whereon the age of the great pharaohs was built.*

121   Daedal

ADJECTIVE

Daedalus was the architect in Greek mythology who designed the labyrinth in Crete to house the beastly Minotaur. *Daedalus* in Latin and Greek means 'skilfully composed or constructed', hence anything daedal (or daedalean) is intricate, clever and complex.

> *He opened the back of the computer and was confronted by a daedal mesh of wires and circuits.*

122   Equivocal

ADJECTIVE

Equivocal, vague and ambiguous all mean 'not clearly understandable' and are used to describe confusing speech or writing. Equivocal – which can be traced back to the Latin prefix *aequi-* ('equi-') and the Latin word *vox* ('voice') – has the specific sense of something that has been deliberately left open to interpretation so that it will deceive or confuse. It therefore carries a subtly negative connotation that the other words lack.

> *The actress gave an equivocal answer when she was asked about her relationship with the leading man.*

123   Chasten

VERB

If you say you would castigate or chastise someone in order to chasten them, you demonstrate a good knowledge of the origin of chasten – all three verbs derive from the Latin verb *castigare*, meaning 'to punish'. (*Castigare* combines Latin *castus*, which means 'pure' and is the source of the English word chaste, with the verb *agere*, meaning 'to lead' or 'to drive'.) Castigate, chastise and chasten share the sense of 'to subject to severe and often physical punishment', but all three verbs are now as likely to refer to a verbal dressing-down as to a physical lesson. Chasten (which arrived in English via the Anglo-French *chastier*) can also be used to mean 'to prune of excess, pretence or falsity'. This led to the more general sense of 'to make more subdued', although the humility can be imposed by a humiliating situation as easily as by a strict taskmaster.

> *He felt suitably chastened by the experience and apologized profusely.*

---

124 Quibble

VERB/NOUN

It is not uncommon for people to use the word quibble to mean a tedious or pedantic argument, like disputing who owes what on a group restaurant bill. Quibble can be used as a verb meaning a small objection or point of order over specific details but can also be (and was originally) used as a noun meaning skirting or ducking away from the main issue.

> *He had a tendency to quibble if confronted with inconvenient truths.*

125 Bombast

NOUN

The original meaning of bombast in English was as a cotton or other material used as padding. It is derived through the Anglo-French *bombés* or *bombace*, from a Medieval Latin word (of various forms, including *bambax* and *bombax*) meaning cotton fibre or wadding. Bombast is no longer used in the sense of stuffing, but the word has been retained in modern English in a figurative sense referring to speech or writing that is stuffed or padded with pretence and unnecessary verbiage.

> *His speeches during the campaign were littered with scaremongering bombast.*

126 Loquacious

ADJECTIVE

The word loquacious derives from the Latin *loqui* meaning 'to speak'. Loquacious differs slightly from near synonyms such as voluble and garrulous in that it implies a sonorous quality of speech, which is why from the word's inception into English in the seventeenth century it was adopted by poets. Soon, loquacious was being used to describe aspects of nature such as the sound of a babbling brook or birdsong. A loquacious speaker usually talks a lot, but often elegantly and engagingly in a soft, resonant voice.

> *He delivered his talk to the audience in a most loquacious manner.*

127 Desultory

ADJECTIVE

First recorded in the English language in 1581 and originating from the Latin *desultorius*, desultory is used to describe something that is lacking definition, purpose or enthusiasm. In Roman times, a *desultor* was a showman whose act was to jump continuously from one horse to another and the word can now be used to describe, for example, a speech or conversation that jumps randomly from one topic to another without any structure or obvious point to it. A performance that is haphazard or unfocused could also be described as desultory.

> *He made a desultory attempt to chat her up but you could tell his heart wasn't in it.*

128 Quietus

NOUN

In feudal times it was common practice to pay tributes to monarchs and wealthy landowners, usually in the form of money. Certain people were exempted from paying this tax for any variety of reasons and so were granted the legal status, in Latin, of being *quietus est*. Gradually, the term was shortened to quietus and could be liberally applied to freedom from the obligation of any outstanding debt. Interestingly, Shakespeare uses the word as a metaphor for death in *Hamlet*: 'For who would bear the whips and scorns of time . . . When he himself might his quietus make / With a bare bodkin?' (*Hamlet*, Act 3, Scene 1) and this meaning of the moment of silence when life fades, although rare, has prevailed. There is also a secondary meaning that developed in the nineteenth century of something that quietens or suppresses.

His family were at his bedside when he met his quietus.

129 Brusque

ADJECTIVE

Brusque originally stems from the Medieval Latin name for butcher's-broom, which was made out of bristly twigs – *bruscus*. The Italian word *brusco*, meaning 'tart', subsequently evolved from *bruscus*, which the French then adopted as *brusque*. The first recorded use of this adjective in English was around 1639, at which time it was used, specifically, to describe the tartness in wine. However, before long, it came to indicate a harsh and stiff manner. Brusque can be employed either to define a notably short, sharp reply or to suggest a forthright, blunt and discourteous way of speaking.

> *The manager appeared to have no favourites among his staff; he treated them all with the same brusque manner.*

130 Emaciated

ADJECTIVE

First recorded in the English language in 1627, emaciated describes a person or creature that is exceptionally thin and weak through hunger, disease or from an eating disorder. An emaciated person could be described as 'wasting away'.

> *During the potato famine, the Irish peasants became emaciated due to the loss of their staple diet.*

131 AND 132 **Propitious** versus **Auspicious**

ADJECTIVES

Propitious is a synonym for auspicious with a slight and subtle change of emphasis. Whereas auspicious suggests something just beginning but which in the future is likely to have a positive outcome, propitious suggests something that has already begun promisingly and where favourable conditions are ongoing. The word is a direct borrow from the Latin *propitious*, which has an identical meaning.

> *The upturn in the economy provided propitious conditions for job creation and rising standards of living.*

> *Meera's career got off to an auspicious start when she won a new client on her first day.*

133 **Valetudinarian**

ADJECTIVE/NOUN

The Latin *valēre* means 'to be strong' and is the root for valour and valiant. It is curious then that valetudinarian describes someone who is sickly or weak. In fact, the Latin word *valetudo* refers to a person's general sense of health and wellbeing, whether positive or negative. By the eighteenth century, however, the word valetudinarian had come to describe only someone in poor health. The adjective form relates to valetudinarian predispositions, which also implies somebody with hypochondriac tendencies.

> *My mother has valetudinarian tendencies; she finds any excuse to go to the doctor.*

134 Nascent

ADJECTIVE

Uncommonly for Latin-derived words, nascent entered into the English language relatively late (mid-seventeenth century). This is curious as it is derived from the word *nasci*, meaning 'to be born', and its close relative *natal* had existed in English for several centuries. Indeed, the Renaissance had come and gone by the time the related word nascent entered into the common lexicon. Something is nascent if it has recently come into existence or is fledgling in terms of time and experience.

> *Her nascent singing career had already started to attract considerable attention from agents and club owners.*

135 Anathema

NOUN

In modern usage, anathema usually relates to something profoundly disliked or loathed, an intolerable state of affairs or situation. Curiously, though, the original use of the word was steeped in religious practice. In ancient Greek, *anathema* was used to describe anything devoted to God. At some point – and etymologists are unsure how or why – the word developed a highly negative connotation. It became a decree passed upon people accused of heresy and was part of the process of excommunication and exile (and no doubt torture and execution in many instances). Both these original meanings have long since diminished and the word is now generally used to describe things we really can't abide.

The thought of spending the whole of Christmas with his overbearing in-laws was complete anathema to him.

❦

136 Querulous

ADJECTIVE

The Latin language is complex, I mean really hard; it seems almost wilfully designed to cause one to whine and complain that it just isn't fair! Take the word querulous, for example – its Latin root is *queri*, meaning 'to complain or gripe'. One would think this is where the word query also comes from but it doesn't – now that is surely something to complain about if you had querulous tendencies and habitually found fault in everything.

The whole holiday was spoiled by a querulous couple who seemed intent on complaining to the hotel staff about even the most trivial of details.

❦

137 Apotheosis

NOUN

In ancient Greek, *apotheosis* meant 'to make into or create a god'. This granting of divine status has come over time to mean placing something on high or, more recently, to hold something up as a perfect model. It can also mean the highest point or most successful example of something.

Nabokov's literary career reached its apotheosis with the publication of Lolita, *the novel that gave him both notoriety and worldwide fame.*

138   Portend

VERB

Portend is used to signify (usually unpleasant) things that are going to happen in the future. The word derives from the Latin verb *portendere,* which means 'to predict or foretell'. Although portend can be used to describe joyous moments – as in 'the bright blue sky portends a great picnic at the beach' – it has a curious negative connotation that everything is going to go wrong.

> *The current impasse in negotiations portends an ultimate financial meltdown for both countries.*

139 AND 140   Abstruse versus Obtuse

ADJECTIVES

The Latin verb *abstrūdere*, meaning 'to conceal', provides the shadowy meaning for abstruse. Something that is abstruse is hard to understand or seemingly deliberately complex. However, obtuse derives from the Latin *obtusus*, which means 'dull or stupid or uncomprehending'. The two words are often confused but it is pretty simple really – obtuse denotes ignorance and abstruse denotes difficulty, often to the detriment of clarity.

> *The abstruse arguments she presented in her lecture baffled the audience.*

> *The seminar paper she presented was riddled with obtuse generalizations.*

141 Assuage

VERB

Of all the lost 'languages', so-called 'Vulgar Latin' is probably the most influential. This was any variant of Latin dialect that creatively formed new words and was spoken informally – in other words the living, evolving version of the language as opposed to the classical, fixed version. The Vulgar Latin term *assuaviare*, meaning 'to sweeten or make pleasant', forms the root of assuage. However, something has to have happened, often something distressing or negative, before it is assuaged.

> *He tried to assuage his guilt over his behaviour by buying his girlfriend some flowers.*

142 Lycanthropic

ADJECTIVE

The word *lycanthropy* comes from the Greek words *lykos,* meaning 'wolf', and *anthropos,* meaning 'human being', and describes the transformation of a person into a werewolf when a full moon swings round. Leaving aside horror films, the adjectival form lycanthropic can be used to describe anyone who is wolfish, manipulative and out for their own rewards.

> *I really don't like the new head of department; he has a lycanthropic air about him.*

143 Mordant

ADJECTIVE

The root of mordant came to modern English through Middle French, ultimately deriving from the Latin verb *mordēre,* which means 'to bite'. In modern idiom, mordant suggests a witty person who can cut you to the quick with a sharp remark. It is a beautiful and much under-used word that sounds nothing like what it actually means.

> *The comedian's comebacks were always mordant and razor sharp.*

144 Orgulous

ADJECTIVE

A proud word in every sense and one that mysteriously dropped out of usage for over two hundred years after Shakespeare's time. To be fine, proud and upstanding is to be orgulous and writers such as W. H. Auden and James Joyce have used this graceful adjective in modern literature.

> *In Troy, there lies the scene. From isles of Greece*
> *The princes orgulous, their high blood chafed,*
> *Have to the port of Athens sent their ships,*
> *[...]*

> WILLIAM SHAKESPEARE, *Troilus and Cressida*,
> The Prologue (*c.* 1600)

145 Fungible

ADJECTIVE

In matters of commerce we all aim to trade like for like, surely? Or maybe get the best arrangement available? So you will need to have a fungible commodity in hand in order to settle the deal. The word fungible derives from the Latin *fungi*, which incidentally has nothing to do with mushrooms but means 'to perform' or 'to action'. Therefore, a fungible commodity is something that can be traded for something else of appropriately equal worth, or a monetary debt to repay.

> *After some haggling online I swapped some rare baseball cards, very fungible in terms of trading, for a vintage 1968 Elvis Comeback Special replica suit.*

146 Behemoth

NOUN

The word behemoth was first recorded in the Bible in the Book of Job and describes a mythical and awesome creature. The word is a direct borrowing from the Hebrew *bĕhēmōth* into Latin and the biblical verses describe the beast hiding in reeds and drinking from the River Jordan, which religious scholars have suggested identifies the creature as a hippopotamus, or possibly an elephant. Over time, the word behemoth has come to be applied to anything that is enormous, awe-inspiring and perhaps a little cumbersome. Russian writer Mikhail Bulgakov chose the word as the name of one of Satan's assassins in his classic novel *The Master and Margarita* (1937). Bulgakov's Behemoth is a sardonic, talking cat who wears a bow tie and walks on his hind legs.

Behold now behemoth, which I made with thee;
he eateth grass as an ox.
Lo now, his strength is in his loins, and his force is
in the navel of his belly.
He moveth his tail like a cedar: the sinews of his
stones are wrapped together.
His bones are as strong pieces of brass; his bones
are like bars of iron.

THE BIBLE, Book of Job, Chapter 40, verses 15–24

147 , 148 AND 149 ## Languid versus Languorous versus Languish

ADJECTIVES/VERB

All three words derive from the Latin *languēre*, meaning 'to languish'. There are, however, subtle differences in the three words' meanings and usage. Languid suggests a lack of vitality brought on by weakness or exhaustion. Languorous is used to describe a person who has made a conscious decision to laze around, basically doing very little. To languish suggests being in a situation, perhaps not of one's own making, that entails a period of time in enforced inactivity or in an unfortunate situation.

> *The heat made her feel languid; she could hardly summon the energy to pour herself a drink.*

> *He spent a languorous morning lying in bed listening to the radio.*

> *After losing his job he languished for almost a year before finding employment.*

79

150 Parlous

ADJECTIVE

Parlous is a word that has slipped in and out of usage in English since the fourteenth century, although increasingly it seems to be coming back into common usage again. Parlous is a synonym for perilous, which arrived in English from the French *perilleus*. Word scholars are unsure why there were two very similar words for the same concept recorded in the fourteenth century, other than that they were just different dialects and spellings of the same word. Parlous, to my mind at least, is the more elegant of the two.

> *The stock market crash had left the country's finances in a parlous state.*

151 Abeyance

ADJECTIVE

Abeyance has both a technical legal meaning and a more figurative usage. The technical term often relates to properties or inheritances – if an estate is in abeyance it means nobody has claimed it, or the rightful claimant has yet to be found. If one's plans for the future are in abeyance, it means they are in place but waiting to be acted upon. The word came into English via the Anglo-French *abair,* which meant 'to open wide'.

> *His plans to go travelling were in abeyance after his father died suddenly.*

152 Hortative

ADJECTIVE

The Latin word *hortari* meant 'to urge' and it is from here that the words 'exhort' and 'hortative' derive – hortative being the adjective describing someone giving advice. Hortative was also at one point used as a noun – to give someone a hortative was basically to lecture them quite sternly about the consequences of their actions, although this usage is rarely deployed today.

> *The document outlined hortative actions in order for the company to move forward.*

153 Vespertine

ADJECTIVE

My cat sleeps a lot during the day due to his vespertine roamings. The Latin word for evening was *vesper*, hence anything vespertine relates to or occurs at night. The adjective vespertillian means bat-like – due to bats' nocturnal habits – and elegant writers and poets have made reference to verspertine shadows creeping across fields and parks at dusk. In Ian Fleming's 1953 novel *Casino Royale*, the character of *femme fatale* Vesper Lynd explains that her parents gave her an unusual name because she was born on a 'dark and stormy night'. The fact that Vesper betrays Bond and breaks his heart is also no doubt related to her shadowy plans.

> *We sat outside in the vespertine dark and listened to the mournful cries of the owl.*

154 Impervious

ADJECTIVE

The English word pervious means accessible although it is fairly rare – interestingly, its antonym impervious is much more common. Both words derive from the Latin word *per*, meaning 'through', as does permeating. Anything described as impervious cannot be penetrated or passed through and the word is also frequently used to describe a stubborn aspect of character.

> *He stared at her blankly, seemingly impervious to her tears and distress.*

❧

155 Mucilaginous

ADJECTIVE

A sticky adjective that oozes off the tongue of pretentious restaurant critics. In a general sense, mucilaginous is anything that secretes or resembles mucilage – a gelatinous substance secreted from certain types of plant life. Mucilage itself derives from the Latin word for mucus, *mucilage*. When used in food reviews it's unlikely the critics are suggesting a dish is mucus-like, but rather they are saying it has a jelly-like or sticky quality.

> *The salad had been dressed in a thin, mucilaginous film of pesto.*

❧

156   Fervid

ADJECTIVE

A very hot and passionate word that comes from the Latin verb *fervēre*, which has the dual meaning of 'to boil' or to seethe or fume about something. Perhaps it's down to the fabled full-blooded Latin temperament that *fervēre* also provides the root for fervent, which is more or less synonymous with fervid. If there is any slight difference in meaning between the two words it is that fervent suggests a long-standing love or belief in something where fervid is more spontaneous and 'of the moment'.

> *She gave a fervid response, rebuking the allegations made against her.*

157   Doughty

ADJECTIVE

It's always nice to find that the origins of a word have persisted from Old English – a highly inflected and complex language that is largely extinct with only a few words still persisting, as roots and traces. The Old English word *dohte* denoted something that has worth and strength and is resilient. As the English language went through its various forms, the word prevailed, although the spelling changed to 'doughty'. It is this hard-headed and irrepressible attitude that sums up the word's meaning.

> *The champion was surprised to come up against such a doughty opponent in the first round of the tournament.*

158 Maieutic

ADJECTIVE

The philosopher Socrates is thought to have first used the Greek word *maieutikos* ('of midwifery') in a figurative sense and provided the root for maieutic. Socrates' mother (at least according to his student Plato as recounted in his *Dialogues*) was a midwife and the great man's founding principles of philosophy, the Socratic method, drew an analogy with a midwife facilitating the birth of a child. For Socrates, new ideas are bought into the world through reasoning and dialogue – they are born through this process. A profound teacher, Socrates believed in teaching using this method (largely involving questioning received wisdom) and encouraging his students to develop their own ideas though dialogue and argument. This method of instruction has become known, since the time of ancient Greece, as maieutic.

> *I had a great teacher at college who practised maieutic techniques in seminars.*

159 Maudlin

ADJECTIVE

Ever wondered why Magdalen/Magdalene Colleges in Oxford and Cambridge Universities are pronounced 'maudlin'? It's because of the Bible, or more specifically, early English translations of the Bible. Mary Magdalene, according to the Christian holy book, was a follower of Jesus who washed his feet with her tears. There is considerable dispute about whether Mary was a devout follower of Christ or a penitent sinner/reformed prostitute (or even the secret wife of Jesus). However, it is the tears that are important here, as to become maudlin is to become sad, excessively so. The link with sin developed much later and the word is often associated with drinking alcohol or being repentant for past misdemeanours. The pronunciation of Magdalen to maudlin occurred during the transitional period in the development of English known as the Great Vowel Shift (between roughly the fourteenth and sixteenth centuries).

> *There is something about watching the leaves fall from the trees that always makes me feel maudlin.*

160   Scurrilous

ADJECTIVE

Doctor Samuel Johnson in his famous *A Dictionary of the English Language* (1755) defines scurrilous as 'using such language as only the licence of a buffoon could warrant.' This is because Johnson traced the word to the Latin *scurra* meaning 'fool or idiot'. Although this initial use of the word – as a description for somebody prone to coarse and vulgar language – prevailed for a while, in modern times scurrilous has come to mean 'containing slanderous accusations or abuse'.

> *The President has constantly railed against the scurrilous abuse he feels he receives from the media.*

161 Gravamen

NOUN

The weight of the world on one's shoulders is a debilitating feeling and this sense of oppressive force pushing down comes from the Latin word *gravis* meaning 'heavy'. The noun gravamen is used technically to identify the part of a particular grievance or complaint that adds weight to an argument. *Gravis* also forms other burdensome and heavy words such as grieve and of course gravity, the force that stops us all floating off into space.

> *The gravamen of the argument rested solely on the premise that the country should have control over its own affairs.*

162 Demiurge

NOUN

A rare and somewhat pompous word borrowed from the Latin *dēmiurgus,* which was in turn borrowed from Greek *dēmiourgós,* and means literally 'master of a craft' or artisan. There is a historical link to Plato's dialogue *Timaeus* – a speculation on the nature of the physical world. In modern usage, a demiurge is an author or creator who has sole responsibility or control over a creative process.

> *There are several notable demiurges working in the field of American television, creating groundbreaking new dramas far in advance of anything the Hollywood studios are currently producing.*

163 Homiletic

ADJECTIVE

To deliver a homily in a place of worship or other gathering is to present a sermon on a theme of moral and ethical importance. This provides the basis for the adjective form homiletic, except a homiletic speech is often viewed quite negatively in modern usage – think of an overly preachy and pious politician banging their own tin drum of self-righteousness.

> *The headmaster's speech to the school at the end of term was homiletic in nature, full of exhortations not to stray from the path of righteousness.*

164 Ingénue

NOUN

William Makepeace Thackeray is often attributed with bringing the word ingénue to the English language via his novel *Vanity Fair*. The word ingenuous (not to be confused with ingenious) has the meaning of somebody innocent and naïve, not attributes that the scheming and manipulative anti-heroine of *Vanity Fair*, Becky Sharp, had in abundance. However, Becky could turn on the wide-eyed charm when it suited a purpose.

> *When attacked sometimes, Becky had a knack of adopting a demure ingénue air, under which she was most dangerous.*
>
> WILLIAM MAKEPEACE THACKERAY, *Vanity Fair* (1848)

165 Apposite

ADJECTIVE

There are various words in English related to the Latin verb *ponere*, meaning 'to place' or 'to put'. The word apposite derives from this and means to place something perfectly, usually in relation to written or spoken language. An apposite phrase or sentence hits the nail on the head; it shows felicity with words.

> *Ayanda's opening speech at the conference was apposite and to the point.*

166 Arriviste

NOUN

In French the verb *arriver* means 'to arrive' and from this the English word arriviste derives. An arriviste is somebody who has suddenly risen to a position of prominence in a particular field. It is often used in the context of the arts to describe somebody newly attracting a lot of publicity or controversy or someone who has seemingly been plucked from obscurity.

> *Winning the Turner Prize cemented his reputation as the arriviste of the Brit-Art scene in the late 1990s.*

167 AND 168 **Impecunious** versus **Pecunious**

ADJECTIVES

The Latin word for money was *pecunia* and from this derived the word pecunious, which for a long time was used to describe somebody wealthy or of good fortune. Over time, this usage has shifted slightly and the use of pecunious adopted a negative context to mean somebody excessively frugal. Impecunious is much more widely used and means to have little or no money or to have fallen on hard times.

> *She was so impecunious she found it increasingly hard to make ends meet.*

> *Bill was renowned for his pecunious ways; he was filthy rich but never so much as tipped a waiter.*

169 **Nuance**

NOUN

A word that literally came from the clouds, as it derives originally from *nubes*, which is the Latin word for cloud. This gave rise to a French term, *nuer*, which meant to create shades of colour. In English, nuance took on the meaning of subtle distinctions or variations and was often used when describing musical compositions. In modern usage, the word subtle is often used with nuance as a modifier, although some pedants would argue this is unnecessary as nuance and subtle mean the same thing.

> *She could tell the subtle nuances of her critique were beyond his comprehension.*

170 **Manifold**

ADJECTIVE

Before the creation of the printing press, books were copied by hand and the verb to describe this process was 'to manifold'. Over time, manifold has become an adjective to describe something either with many facets or marked by many variations. It is often used in a negative context to describe a glut of problems or issues.

> *The manifold issues with the company's finances were mounting up.*

171 **Pluvial**

ADJECTIVE

In the seventeenth and eighteenth centuries, priests wore long raincoats known as pluvials to protect them from inclement weather when going about their duties, from the Latin word for rain, *pluvia*. Pluvial has come to describe anything related to rainfall, such as pluvial streams or pluvial seasons.

> *The months of April and May are the pluvial seasons and account for over half the island's annual rainfall.*

172 **Guerdon**

NOUN

A rare word that has a quite esteemed literary history dating back to Chaucer. To receive guerdon was to gain a reward or recompense for an action. Shakespeare makes a joke on the word in *Love's Labour's Lost* when Costard

the fool is given money to deliver love letters and says
that receiving guerdon is much better than remuneration
(when of course they amount to the same thing):

> *Guerdon, O sweet guerdon! Better than*
> *remuneration; eleven-pence farthing better: most*
> *sweet guerdon!*

> WILLIAM SHAKESPEARE, *Love's Labour's Lost*, Act 3,
> Scene 1 (*c.* 1594)

173 Flagitious

ADJECTIVE

In Latin, *flagitium* was something wicked or shameful and
this also provides the root for flagellate, meaning to flog –
probably as supposedly wicked and shameful people were
whipped for their crimes and misdemeanours. These days
something described as flagitious is marked by scandal
or disgrace or something related to a vice such as sexual
promiscuity.

> *It seemed clear to the judge that the defendant's*
> *flagitious crimes should be given the highest penalty.*

174 Delitescent

ADJECTIVE

One of those words that means something markedly
different from how it sounds. One could be forgiven
for assuming that delitescent had some relationship to
delightful or delicate. In fact it has no connection to either
of those words. The Latin verb *delitescere*, meaning 'to hide

or conceal', provides the source for delitescent. Anything that is wilfully or slyly concealed can be described with this word.

> *The delitescent nature of the report means that the full details of the investigation are unlikely to be made public.*

❧

175 Mellifluous
ADJECTIVE

We have bees to thank for the elegant adjective mellifluous. In Latin, *mel* means honey and the verb *fluere* means to flow, hence something mellifluous flows like honey. The word is used figuratively, of course, and often associated with music and voices. Be careful not to confuse it with melliferous, which is usually used to describe plants that can be pollinated by insects and therefore produce honey.

> *His mellifluous tones were in high demand for use in television advertisements.*

❧

176 Ordure
NOUN

A somewhat graceful term for something pretty unpleasant. Ordure derives from an identical Middle French word for filth and waste, particularly human or animal excrement, and its root lies in the Latin word for horrid, *horridus*. The word is used figuratively to describe moral decay or things that are degenerating into a state of filth and degradation.

The lack of effective sanitation systems meant that after the floods the street were strewn with human ordure.

∾

177 Shibboleth

NOUN

The word shibboleth derives from the Hebrew word for stream and is a direct borrowing from the Bible. In the Book of Judges, it is a test word to distinguish two tribes who are at war, and when the word first came into English it took on the meaning of a military code word. Over time, the definition has changed and shibboleth has taken on a variety of different meanings. The most common usage is to describe a widely held belief or idea, which may be a signifier of a particular group – such as 'a shibboleth of the working classes'. More negatively, a shibboleth can also be an oft-repeated truism or platitude that many people believe has little or no foundation in actual truth.

> *She repeated the old shibboleth that time heals all wounds.*

∾

178 Repine

VERB

The Old English word *pinian* had the meaning of 'to suffer' and people certainly do suffer when they repine. The word is more or less synonymous with 'to pine' in the sense of longing for something lost. If there is a distinction it is that pining has the sense of deep sorrow, whereas to repine is to feel discontented or hard done by whatever it is that has been lost.

> *He had a tendency to repine over missed chances and lost opportunities.*

❦

179 Risible

ADJECTIVE

In Latin, *ridēre* means 'to laugh' and originally risible meant something laughter-inducing. This could be a risible remark, as in a quip or a joke, or a risible situation. In modern usage, however, risible has become darker in tone as the world has become more cynical. Risible is these days almost always used in negative contexts for something so pitiful it attracts scorn.

> *The author complained about the risible sum he was offered by his publishers.*

❦

180 Saporific

ADJECTIVE

When we eat a fine meal at a restaurant we savour the flavours. Saporific is a descriptive word for anything that excites the taste buds and derives from the Latin verb *sapor*, meaning to savour.

> *The chef had produced a masterful signature dish with the perfect balance of saporific flavours and seasoning.*

❦

181 Febrile

ADJECTIVE

Febrile was originally used as a medical term for conditions brought on, or characterized, by fever – hence the febrile stage of an illness. The word derives from the Latin word for fever, *febris*. Febrile can also be used figuratively to describe feverish emotions or the heated atmosphere of a large crowd.

> *The febrile atmosphere at recent political rallies has seen journalists and newscasters abused and assaulted.*

182 Circumspect

ADJECTIVE

Circumspect derives from a compound of two Latin words, the word for 'round' (*circum*) and 'to look' (*specere*). This gives the sense that to be circumspect is to survey a situation and weigh up all possibilities before making a decision. It is often used synonymously with cautious, although the latter word suggests a general reluctance to do something rather than the tendency to examine the possibilities before acting.

> *He was always circumspect in his business dealings.*

183 Chary

ADJECTIVE

Chary is an adjective that has had several meanings in English through time. Originally, the word (derived from

Old English *caru*) meant to be sorrowful. By the sixteenth century, however, it had come to mean 'cherished' and 'dearest'. Both of these meanings have long been lost and in modern usage a chary person is someone who is cautious or hesitant to get involved in a particular situation or issue.

> *The government was chary in its response to the growing tensions in the south of the country.*

⁓

184 Fainéant

NOUN/ADJECTIVE

It should come as no surprise that fainéant is a direct borrowing from the French *fait-nient*, which means 'does nothing'. A fainéant is a rather quaint term for idlers and loafers but with the emphasis that the person in question has chosen to live their life that way. In nineteenth-century France, a group of literary types called the *flâneurs* embraced the fainéant lifestyle. A *flâneur* is someone who strolls the streets observing society.

> *It was not uncommon for the wealthy aristocrats of nineteenth-century France to frequent the cafés and salons as part of their fainéant lifestyle.*

⁓

185 Filial

ADJECTIVE

The bond between a parent and a child is defined as a filial relationship. The Latin word for son is *filius* and daughter *filia* but in English there is no distinction between the genders and filial applies to both sexes. The adjective can also be used in a more general sense to describe the relationship between something old and something recently created or born.

> *I was lucky to have been bought up in a family where the filial relationships were strong and loving.*

❧

186 Lentitude

ADJECTIVE

Derived from the Latin word for slowness (*lentus*), lentitude is a word that has resurfaced in English after falling out of usage during the late twentieth century. Lentitude describes a certain type of sluggishness and apathy that is usually brought on by reluctance to complete an action.

> *He displays considerable lentitude when faced with his homework as he would clearly rather be playing video games.*

❧

187 Sententious

ADJECTIVE

A sententious person is someone who excessively moralizes in the belief that they are ethically superior. This has not always been the case, however, as originally the word sententious meant something full of meaning like a maxim or aphorism. It is a shame this sense has been lost and that nowadays the implication of being sententious is simply pomposity.

> *I loathe watching that man interviewed on the television as he spouts sententious claptrap.*

188 Decimate

VERB

Decimate is a problem word – that is to say, a word that has strayed from its original meaning and one that causes a small group of etymologists and linguists to get quite hot under the collar. The origins of the word lie in Ancient Rome, where it was a common practice to quell mutinies in the military by executing one tenth of the rebellious legion. Hence, to decimate actually means to reduce something by 10 per cent, not to lay it to waste or destroy it completely. Sentences such as: 'Budget cuts to local government have decimated public services' only hold true if the services have been reduced by 10 per cent. Most people, however, would assume that there were hardly any services left.

The spread of the virus decimated the population, reducing it by nearly 10 per cent.

❧

189 Deprecate

VERB

The origins of deprecate lie in religion and the power of prayer. Originally derived from the Latin *deprecari,* meaning 'to pray against' something, the verb 'to deprecate' meant to try to stop or avert something by appealing to God. Sometime in the eighteenth century the meaning shifted to its modern sense of 'to express disapproval, belittle or disparage'. There is also a secondary meaning that encompasses the idea of playing something down or showing deliberate modesty, as in self-deprecating. The original meaning of deprecate still survives in theological circles.

She speaks five languages fluently but deprecates her abilities.

190 AND 191 Disputatious versus Disputable

ADJECTIVES

Disputatious can be applied both to people and to things, such as issues or ideas. We have all met people who could start an argument in an empty house, so to speak, and these are people with disputatious character traits. A disputatious notion, concept or issue is by extension something likely to start an argument and/or is considered controversial. The word should not be confused with its near relative disputable, which merely means open to question. Both words derive from the same Latin root but disputable is closer in meaning to its ancestor *disputare*, which meant 'to discuss'.

> *There is a guy who drinks in my local bar who is so disputatious he'll argue about anything.*

> *Much of the evidence presented in court was highly disputable.*

192 AND 193 Flagrant versus Blatant

ADJECTIVES

The Latin word *flagrans* had the meaning of something that was burning or fiery and originally in English flagrant had the same meaning: 'The flagrant sun beat down upon his brow'. By the 1800s, the word had changed its meaning to its current usage of an action or actions conspicuously wrong or immoral. Presumably such actions were believed to result in the perpetrator burning in hell, hence the fiery connection. There is an argument that flagrant and blatant are not interchangeable for this reason. Blatant suggests an error or obvious mistake that has attracted disapproving attention. Flagrant is much worse and denotes a lack of morality and/or deliberate wrongdoing.

> *The flagrant abuses of power over several years eventually caused his downfall.*

> *The blatant foul in the sixty-third minute of the game resulted in the home team being reduced to ten men.*

∽

194 Ebullient

ADJECTIVE

Originally, ebullient (which derives from the Latin *ebullire*) was used to describe something bubbling, like a pot boiling on a stove. Over time, the word has come to describe people who are enthusiastic and bubbly in their disposition.

> *She has such an ebullient personality she lights up any social occasion.*

∽

195 Amalgamate

VERB

Ever been to the dentist with a sore tooth and ended up having it filled? The likelihood is the dentist used an *amalgam* of liquid mercury and a metal alloy. The word amalgam, to mean the result of blending these two substances together, has existed in English since the fifteenth century – a time when all sorts of dubious experimental science took place and alchemy was all the rage. Over time, the verb 'to amalgamate' developed a more general usage to describe any single compound produced by combining two or more elements.

The company, in order to cut costs, has decided to amalgamate two departments into a single unit.

196 Dilemma

NOUN

A dilemma, linguistic purists insist, should only consist of two options both of which are not particularly satisfactory or appealing. The phrase 'to be caught on the horns of a dilemma' illustrates this definition. The expression is not, as might be assumed, related to the devil but refers to a rhetorical device mentioned in the works of Dutch scholar Erasmus (1466–1536). This involves presenting your opponent with two options, both of which will lead them to lose the argument – so no matter which option they go for, they will run into the sharp point of a horn. In modern usage, however, people often talk of dilemmas being much more positive.

I'm in a dilemma about whether to go to the party or stay in and watch a film.

197 Dichotomy

NOUN

Traditionally, a dichotomy was something that could be divided into two distinct groups or concepts that are contradictory or opposing, such as heaven and hell. This has led to the idea of dichotomy meaning two things that are opposed to each other, such as the dichotomy between communism and capitalism or good and evil. The phrase 'a false dichotomy' concerns a situation where two seemingly contradictory choices are presented when in fact there are other options available.

> *The smaller political groups have long battled against the false dichotomy of the two-party state.*

❧

198 Ideologue

NOUN

Ideologue is a direct borrowing from the French *idéologue*, which is used to describe someone who adheres to a particular political or religious ideology. In English, the word has a more negative connotation as somebody who blindly adheres to an ideology – a militant who is inflexible and stubborn in their views.

> *There is concern that the hawkish ideologues at the extreme wing of the party are doing irreparable damage to hopes of gaining power.*

❧

199 Forensic

ADJECTIVE

Forensic is an example of that modern phenomenon whereby the literal meaning of a word is abused or misunderstood and, once this error has taken grip, the mistake rapidly becomes part of contemporary parlance. Forensic derives from the Latin *forensis*, meaning 'public', which in turn came from *forum*, meaning 'a place of gathering'. The adjective forensic originally meant 'belonging to or appropriate for a court of law'. The term forensic science therefore is scientific evidence gathered for the purposes of the legal proceedings. At some point in the late twentieth century, the media started using forensic to mean rigorous and detailed in relation to an examination or argument. Politicians started putting forth forensic arguments and universities conducted forensic research projects. None of these uses, strictly speaking, is correct unless the information gathered is to be used in a court of law.

> *Although initially convicted, the defendant was released on appeal after new forensic evidence came to light.*

~~~

200 AND 201   Foment versus Ferment

VERBS

The earliest documented uses of the verb foment appear in medical texts offering advice on how to soothe various aches and pains by the application of moist heat. Foment can be traced to the Latin verb *fovēre*, which means simply to apply heat to something. However, within a century of the first original recorded use of the word, a metaphorical meaning appeared. Foment retains a sense of heating something up, but these days it means to rouse or incite and is usually used in the context of riots and rebellions. The word is not to be confused with ferment, which only relates to making bread or alcohol by mixing ingredients with yeast.

> *His rousing speech was blamed for fomenting the subsequent riots.*

> *Tyler was fermenting a fearsome home-brew in the cupboard under the stairs.*

~~~

202 Pristine

ADJECTIVE

The Latin word *pristinus*, from which pristine derives, meant early or original in form and had nothing to do with cleanliness or otherwise. Perhaps it was through nostalgia that pristine took on the meaning of something clean, fresh and most importantly unsullied, which is the sense in which it is used today.

> *I went out and bought myself a pristine white shirt to wear to the wedding.*

203 and 204 Venal versus Venial

ADJECTIVES

Two words with vastly different meanings separated by a single vowel. To commit a venal act is basically to accept or administer a bribe and follows the old adage that everything has a price. In many countries, venal acts are regarded as corruption and if exposed would likely entail some form of punishment or sanction. To commit a venial act is to do something careless but largely trivial and so the culprit will most likely be pardoned or forgiven. Venal derives from the Latin *venum*, which simply meant something for sale; whereas venial descends from *venia* meaning favour or pardon. It is highly likely that Latin speakers also got confused between the two words.

> *His venal activities had begun to attract the attention of the police.*

> *It was decided that the offence was venial in nature and a full pardon was issued.*

205 Horripilate

VERB

This word essentially came into public circulation via nineteenth-century gothic novels, although it had an obscure usage in medical circles prior to that. To horripilate is to have goose bumps or to undergo the sensation of hairs standing up on the back of one's neck. Gothic writers used the word descriptively to build tension and excitement, although in medical terms the word relates more to the feeling of shivering through illness or fever.

> *At the height of his illness he felt extreme chills, which caused him to horripilate.*

206 Perfunctory

ADJECTIVE

To do something in a perfunctory manner is to do something with little care or attention. It is a direct borrowing from the Latin *perfunctorius*, which has an identical meaning. Perfunctory can be applied mostly to actions done with little enthusiasm but can also be applied to tedious or unnecessary routines.

> *Helen gave the room a perfunctory clean before her mother came round.*

207 AND 208 **Enormity** versus **Enormousness**

NOUNS

Another bugbear of lexicographers is the use and misuse of the word enormity. The argument goes that enormity doesn't mean great size but traditionally means something extremely vicious, wicked and immoral ('enormousness' is the proper word for something large). On the night President Obama was elected President of the United States he spoke in his acceptance address of the 'enormity of the tasks' that lay ahead. This wasn't an announcement that he was about to carry out some evil and reprehensible acts – he just meant he had a lot of work to do. Enormity, of course, is used in the context of something huge all the time in common speech and eventually the two words, although different in meaning, will become completely synonymous and the original meaning of enormity will be lost.

> *The enormity of the crime shocked the whole nation.*

> *The enormousness of Sadie's new sofa was going to cause a problem in her new house.*

209 **Inchoate**

ADJECTIVE

We all have big plans, hopes and ideas for the future. The modern term 'Bucket List' sums up the meaning of inchoate. In Latin, *inchoare* means 'to start work' on something or describes something to be worked on. There is a slight sense in this word, however, that these half-formed notions may never come to full fruition or be realized.

She suddenly realized inchoate feelings of affection for a man who, up till now, she had thought of only as a friend.

❧

210 Ineffable

ADJECTIVE

Ineffable comes from the Latin *ineffabilis*, meaning 'incapable of being expressed'. The word is sometimes used to describe taboos or things that should not be discussed. The word is often thought of as a synonym of unspeakable but this is not the case. An unspeakable act, for example, is something so awful there are no words for it. An ineffable sunset, however, is one of such striking beauty it cannot be described. An ineffable subject is one that can be spoken about but most right-minded people prefer not to discuss, such as toilet habits.

There was something totally ineffable about the performance; it transcended words.

❧

211 Jeremiad

NOUN

A jeremiad is a prolonged complaint or bugbear and/or a lamentation about suffering. The word is thought to derive from the Old Testament's Book of Jeremiah. The Hebrew prophet is known for his austere and sombre admonitions against his own people for their false values and bad faith. In the eighteenth century, the name Jeremiah became a slang term for a naysayer of pious character and it is from this that the noun jeremiad developed as a term for a long-standing grievance or objection.

There is a long-standing jeremiad against elite universities for doing little to provide places for students from under-privileged backgrounds.

༺ஒ༻

212 Malapert

ADJECTIVE

As with many words in English (see maladroit on page 29), the prefix *mal-* meaning 'bad' gives the clue to the meaning of this adjective. The Middle English word *apert*, which was the word for 'openness', then provides the definition. In short, someone who is malapert is brash and bold to the point of being obnoxious. Shakespeare was particularly fond of the word and used it several times, most notably (and ironically) in *Twelfth Night*, where the unashamedly malapert Sir Toby Belch accuses Sebastian of being impudent.

> *What, what? Nay, then I must have an ounce or two of this malapert blood from you.*
>
> WILLIAM SHAKESPEARE, *Twelfth Night*, Act 4, Scene 1 (*c.* 1601)

༺ஒ༻

213 AND 214 Proscribe versus Prescribe

VERBS

Another pair of words with very similar spellings that are often confused. Proscribe is probably the more uncommon of the two and means to ban or outlaw something in an official way. Prescribe has a common medical usage, whereby a doctor prescribes a particular treatment or medicine, but it also has a more general use to mean recommending a particular course of action, usually with some power or authority.

> *Many European nations proscribe and even criminalize various forms of hate speech.*

> *The doctor prescribed some sleeping tablets to try and combat my insomnia.*

❧

215 Peremptory

ADJECTIVE

Peremptory people like to be obeyed, they are brusque and high-handed. There is also a suggestion that any peremptory orders are to be complied with immediately and without question. This has led to the word often being used in legal jargon to mean something which cannot be disputed or appealed against, such as a peremptory order or sanction – a peremptory reprimand would imply a severe sanction without cause to appeal.

> *His faux pas on social media gave his employers no option other than peremptory dismissal.*

❧

216 Verdant

ADJECTIVE

A graceful word that has been used in English as a synonym for green since the sixteenth century. Verdant is most commonly used to describe lush, green pastures and parklands although it has a secondary meaning that is also long established. Young thoroughbred racehorses are often described as 'running green' early in their racing careers

– meaning they are showing their rawness or immaturity. Verdant can therefore be used to describe anything that lacks experience or is in the process of developing and growing.

> *The meadow that stretched out before her was lush and verdant.*

❧

217 **Nomenclature**

NOUN

One of the bugbears of the famous English lexicographer Henry Watson Fowler (1858–1933) was the misuse of the word nomenclature. In general usage it is merely a rather highbrow synonym for a name of something or someone. Fowler, however, contended that as the word is derived directly from the Latin *nomenclatura,* it should only mean 'a system of naming things'. The fact that it is a noun is somewhat ironic either way you look at it and quite what this system of naming things actually comprises is anybody's guess outside of medicine and the sciences, where it is most commonly used in Fowler's sense. Nomenclature has, however, been used to mean name, usually a proper noun, since the seventeenth century.

> *Botany draws heavily upon Latin for its nomenclature of different species.*

❧

218 AND 219 **Scruple** versus **Unscrupulous**

NOUN/ADJECTIVE

The Latin word *scrupus*, meaning 'a sharp pebble', is the root of the word scruple. Roman statesman and philosopher Cicero (106–43 BC) is credited with using the word metaphorically to mean an issue that is a cause of uneasiness or a question of conscience. In the traditional sense, then, a scruple is an ethical dilemma. Over time, however, it has come to be used in terms of a set of rules or moral code. Unscrupulous has come to mean somebody ruthless and without morals, when it should actually refer to somebody free from the emotional stress of any moral strife.

> *My father had strict scruples when it came to matters concerning politeness and good manners.*

> *The unscrupulous behaviour of a small cabal of aggressive businessmen robbed the town of its chance of prosperity.*

220 **Solicitude**

NOUN

To have solicitude for others is a fine and noble quality that cynics would say is rare in the harsh modern world. Although feeling solicitude means to feel agitated and anxious on a base level, the implication is that this concern is for the plight of another person or group of people. The word encompasses a sense of wanting to offer care and protection and the overriding feeling that the suffering of others is something we should all do our best to alleviate.

> *I felt tremendous solicitude for the refugees risking life and limb fleeing from a war zone, only to be caged in camps.*

221 **Laconic**

ADJECTIVE

Laconia was a region of ancient Greece, home to the fearless Spartans. For several centuries, laconic referred to anything related to the Spartan clan. The Spartans were proud and didn't mince their words, so became known as being rather abrupt and to the point. The modern meaning of laconic derives from this reputation and relates to terseness and a concise use of words. The word is often misused to mean laid back but it is explicitly the use of language, in either speech or written form, to which laconic should refer.

> *I'm always slightly unnerved by the laconic emails I receive from my old friend Jim; they are terse and lack warmth.*

222 AND 223 **Oblige** versus **Obligate**

VERBS

Now here is a curious conundrum: two words descended from the same Latin root – *obligare* meaning 'to bind or tie to' – and yet with very different meanings in modern usage. One thing they do have in common is that both words are frequently used in their past participle forms of obliged and obligated. Although originally both had a legal connection in that the meanings were closely 'tied to' being bound or constrained by law or duty, over time obligate has become heavy with the woes of the world and the millstone of duty and responsibility. Oblige, on the other hand, has developed a much more positive usage – encompassing a sense that people actually like doing favours for other people ('much obliged').

Lord and Lady Snodgrass-Smythe would be most obliged if you would kindly accept an invitation to their daughter Tamara's wedding.

We all have a moral obligation to protect the environment for the sake of future generations.

❧

224 Lagniappe

NOUN

An uncommon word that American writer and man of letters Mark Twain (1835–1910) was most taken with. In his *Life on the Mississippi* (1883), Twain describes discovering the word in New Orleans in the French Quarter, where it was customary for traders to give a small gift or a lagniappe to generous customers. The word derives from Louisiana Creole, a hybrid of various languages with standard French as its base. Louisiana Creole is a dying language, sadly, with recent estimates claiming it is spoken by less than 10,000 people in Louisiana, which has a population of almost five million.

We spent a small fortune in the artisan shops around the French Quarter buying souvenirs but every trader furnished us with a lagniappe to show their appreciation.

❧

225 Lamentable

ADJECTIVE

Lamentable is a dual-purpose word as it means almost its antonym depending on the context. Originally, lamentable meant sorrow-inducing, and was used to describe something mourned because it was lost. However, at some point in the nineteenth century, people seemed to become more cynical about human suffering and thus lamentable came to be something pitiful, pathetic and deserving of scorn. What is extraordinary is that both meanings have survived although the original meaning is rarely used.

> *His film shone a spotlight on the lamentable casualties of war.*

> *His lamentable efforts to chat-up women were legendary among his peers.*

226 AND 227 Egoism versus Egotism

NOUNS

Listen to me. I say that there is a difference between egotism and egoism and I'm the author so therefore I am always right. That last sentence could be described as an example of egotism, which can be typically characterized by an excessive use of the singular personal pronoun 'I'. Although not quite a direct translation, egotism is a borrowing from an identical word in Late Anglo-Latin, which actually described idiot-like personality traits. Egoism, on the other hand, is different in that egoism is actually almost a doctrine whereby people believe that self-interest is the major motivating force behind human nature. People who are egotists are show-offs, braggarts and incurious about anyone but themselves, although they are usually foolish and not as popular as they think. People who embrace egoism are frankly quite scary and probably not to be trusted.

His rampant egotism is unbelievable. I thrashed him at golf but he claims he let me win.

The egoism of some politicians becomes ruthlessly apparent as their grip on power starts to slip.

228 AND 229 **Constrain** versus **Restrain**

VERBS

Many people get confused by these two words but it is really just a matter of cause and effect. Something is restrained to stop it from occurring but something is constrained to stop it getting any better, but most likely worse. Both words have the sense of physical force being the major agent but people can be constrained by abstract forces too, such as class, creed, gender or race.

There are many social and economic factors that constrain the number of working-class entrants to the top universities.

After being pelted with an egg, the politician had to be restrained by security guards from attacking his assailant.

230 **Latitant**

ADJECTIVE

Latitant is another word concerning concealment, which could be used to describe somebody hiding away for some reason. Latitant in zoology relates to any animal that hibernates in the winter, such as hedgehogs or bears.

I'm sure my friend Phil has latitant tendencies as he barely goes out during the winter months.

231 AND 232   **Lethe** versus **Lethonomia**

NOUNS

In Classical Greek, the word *lethe* means 'oblivion', 'forgetfulness' or 'concealment'. In Greek mythology, the River Lethe is in Hades, the underworld, and drinking its waters causes people to forget their past sins and misdemeanours and enter into a state of insensibility. In *Hamlet*, the ghost of his father exhorts the young prince of Denmark not to fall into apathy but avenge his death:

> *I find thee apt,*
> *And duller shouldst thou be than the fat weed*
> *That roots itself in ease on Lethe wharf*
> *Wouldst thou not stir in this.*

> WILLIAM SHAKESPEARE, *Hamlet*, Act 1, Scene 5
> (*c.* 1599)

Lethe in English is an old-fashioned word for forgetfulness. Lethonomia, drawing upon the medical profession's penchant for Latinate terms and classical allusions, is the inability to remember names.

> *My father has dementia and the one thing that really seems to have affected him the most is the lethonomia – he can't remember the name for anything much any more.*

⌒⌒⌒

233 **Abjure**

VERB

Abjure has its roots in the Latin word *jurare* meaning 'to swear' and the prefix *ab-* meaning 'away', hence 'to swear away'. There is an implication that when someone abjures something they are recanting or renouncing a previously held belief in something, such as abjuring faith in a religion or doctrine.

> *Mary had been brought up in the Catholic faith, but abjured Christianity after she lost her husband in a terrible accident.*

⁓

234 **Litotes**

NOUN

In mathematics, if two negatives are added together they produce a positive. In grammar, the use of double negatives in writing is a thorny and contentious issue, some grammarians get very hot under the collar about it yet they are not uncommon in figures of speech – and this is where litotes comes into the argument. Litotes is the word for a rhetorical device of defining or affirming something by its contrary or negative. There are numerous examples of litotes in everyday language and culture, from statements such as 'it's *not unusual* for the weather to be changeable in England in summer' to *The Rolling Stones* song 'I Can't Get No Satisfaction'. Litotes adds colour and a rhetorical flourish to speech and writing.

> *It's not uncommon to have tropical storms in the Caribbean.*

⁓

235   Polyptoton

NOUN

My daughter is named Polly – this was more by accident than design and ironic in a way, as *poly* in Latin means 'many' and she is an only child. Polyptoton, an extremely hard word to say, is another rhetorical device involving repetition of a word in a different case, inflection or voice in the same sentence. It is much beloved by romantic poets such as Wordsworth and Alfred Lord Tennyson – at base a form of literary stutter; at best a clever little twist, as in the first line of the following example.

> *My own heart's heart, my ownest own, farewell;*
> *It is but for a little space I go:*
> *And ye meanwhile far over moor and fell*
> *Beat to the noiseless music of the night!*

ALFRED LORD TENNYSON, 'I Have Led her Home, My Love, My Only Friend, *Maud* (1855)

236   Canard

NOUN

There is an old French saying, *vendre des canards à moitié*, which means 'to half-sell ducks'. The expression was used to describe something that was a trick or a deception and led to the French word for duck entering into English to describe a hoax or a lie. The word canard is often used to describe false reports or seemingly deliberate distortions of the truth, often by manipulation of data and statistics. Canard is also used in aeronautics to describe particular aspects of aircraft design.

> *The whole story was a canard, riddled with misinformation and falsehood.*

237 Bedlam

NOUN

In 1247, Simon FitzMary, the Sheriff of London, founded
a priory at Bishopsgate, providing both the land and the
funding. By the fourteenth century, this priory had a hospital
devoted to the medical needs of the poor of London and was
called the Hospital of St Mary of Bethlehem. Over time, the
hospital developed into a specialist centre for treating the
mentally ill, although in truth this probably amounted to
little more than incarcerating the poor wretches in chains
and using various means of torture to keep them under
control. When Henry VIII dissolved the monasteries in 1536,
the priory was given to the city of London and made into a
royal foundation for the care and protection of the insane.
The word bedlam is thought to be a local dialect contraction
of the name of the hospital Bethlehem. A curious public
fascination with the mentally ill led to the hospital charging
a small entrance fee for visitors to view the patients chained
in their cells. The noise of the screaming, howling patients
then led to the word bedlam being used to describe any
noisy commotion or state of disorder.

> *It was complete bedlam in the classroom as the
> young teacher struggled to control his unruly
> students.*

238 Nepotism

NOUN

The word nepotism derives from the Italian word *nipote*
meaning nephew. In 1667, Italian historian and satirist
Gregorio Leti (1630–1701) published a scandalous book
entitled *Il Nepotismo di Roma*, which roughly translates

as *Nepotism in Rome*. Leti's book chronicled various disreputable and corrupt acts by a succession of Popes, including the practice of promoting family members to high-ranking positions in the church. As Popes were supposed to be sworn to celibacy, any illegitimate children they fathered were often passed off (according to Leti) as being nephews. Leti's book was popular in English translation, perhaps because it was a damning indictment of the corruption of the Catholic church in Rome and led to the word nepotism entering into English to describe special favours being bestowed upon family members by people in positions of power or influence.

> *She got her position as political editor entirely through nepotism.*

239 Rigmarole

NOUN

In the Middle Ages, *ragman* was the name of a popular parlour game in which a series of humorous or scurrilous character descriptions written in verse were rolled up in scrolls and participants would take it in turns to choose a random scroll and read out its contents. The scroll was called a *ragman roll* and is thought to derive from the French verse folk tales of a fictional King named Rageman Le Bon (Rageman the Good), which date back to the thirteenth century. Over time, a ragman roll came to refer to lists of objects in an inventory and gradually acquired the meaning of something tedious and meaningless – probably reflecting the monotony of compiling or reading lists. By the eighteenth century, the word changed again to rigmarole and was used to describe long-winded or over-complicated discourse in speech and writing. The modern sense of the word retains this sense of something being tiresome, as rigmarole is usually applied to long and unnecessarily complicated procedures.

The rigmarole of filling out these forms seems designed entirely to frustrate and confuse claimants.

240 Maroon

VERB

In American Spanish in the sixteenth and seventeenth centuries, the word *cimarrón* related to the slave trade in the Spanish colonies in the West Indies. A *cimarrón* was a word used to describe a slave who escaped from his masters and lived wild in the uninhabited mountains or forests. The word was borrowed first into French and abbreviated as *marron* and then into English as maron, also meaning an escaped slave living a feral life. This was the golden age of the pirate and privateer, however, and the verb 'to maroon' began to appear in English to describe somebody abandoned and left to their own devices – a common punishment among buccaneers and so called because the unfortunate victim was left to live like a maron. In modern English it means anything trapped or abandoned with little chance of escape.

After the volcanic eruption in Iceland in 2010, many air passengers were marooned in airports across Europe.

241 AND 242   **Locution** versus **Eloquent**

NOUN/ADJECTIVE

The Latin word *loquī*, meaning 'to speak', provides the root for many words in English relating to speech and language, such as loquacious and ventriloquist. Locution and eloquent are also derived from this Latin stem. Locution describes a particular form of expression or a peculiarity of phrasing, especially a word or expression characteristic of a region, group or cultural level. Eloquent means 'spoken fluently', though over time, fluency with words wasn't enough and eloquent has developed an extended meaning of speaking expressively and is also sometimes used to describe artworks (music, paintings or literature) or even architecture.

> *The curious locution of the Deep South vernacular can be confusing to travellers.*

> *The novel came to be viewed as an eloquent expression of the discontent and turmoil of the Great Depression.*

243   **Circumlocution**

NOUN

In Charles Dickens' *Little Dorrit*, the character Mr Clennam encounters the Circumlocution Office – a department of state whose sole purpose is to create confusion by tying red tape to red tape; forms need to be filled out merely to request permission to fill out more forms. The word circumlocution means evasiveness in speech or simply talking around a subject without being specific or precise. Dickens clearly felt that government departments and the civil service obstructed more than they served.

Whatever was required to be done, the Circumlocution Office was beforehand with all the public departments in the art of perceiving – HOW NOT TO DO IT.

CHARLES DICKENS, *Little Dorrit* (1857)

⌘

244 Longanimity

NOUN

Longanimity has been in English since the mid-fifteenth century and derives from the Latin word *longanimis*, meaning 'patient'. To have the capacity for longanimity means to exhibit forbearance of misfortune, especially in unfortunate circumstances, such as long-term illness or injury.

She displayed terrific longanimity whilst undergoing treatment for cancer.

⌘

245 Lucubration

NOUN

The compiling of this book has involved lucubrations: painstaking, laborious and intense periods of study. The word derives from the Latin *lucubrare*, meaning 'to study by lamp or candlelight', and is redolent of working through the night on something with feverish concentration.

She was exhausted by the lucubrations involved in revising for her final exams.

⌘

246   Maculated

ADJECTIVE

Maculate has been in English since the fourteenth century and derives from the Latin *maculāre*, meaning 'to stain or blemish'. Around the time the word first appeared, spots, blemishes or lesions on the skin were among the symptoms of the Black Death, so for someone to become spotted (maculated) was usually very bad news. The word also has a secondary meaning to become besmirched or blemished by something.

> *His reputation has been maculated by the scandalous claims in the newspapers.*

247   Intransigent

ADJECTIVE

In Spain in the eighteenth century, the term *Los Intransigentes* was applied to radical political parties in the Spanish Cortes, the legislative assembly. The original *Los Intransigentes* were left-wing radicals, but by the time the Spanish monarchy was overthrown in 1873 the term was used to describe radical republicans. It was around this time that the anglicized intransigent came into English, originally to describe political stubbornness. The antonym *transigent* exists in English also, meaning willing to compromise, although this is rarely used in print.

> *The complex negotiations hit a roadblock due to the intransigent parties being unwilling to find a compromise.*

248 AND 249   **Quotient** versus **Quota**

NOUNS

Middle English *quocient* derives from the Latin *quot,* meaning 'how much/many'. From here the word quotient developed in the field of mathematics in the fifteenth century to describe the resulting figure from one number being divided by another. It is often mistakenly used by people who assume quotient is a rather posh synonym for quota – it isn't (though this meaning is becoming increasingly accepted nowadays). A quota is an amount or proportional share of something. Interestingly, quota came into English a century after quotient and derives from the Latin *quota pars*, meaning 'how great a part'.

> *Five is the quotient of ten divided by two.*

> *The strict fishing quotas imposed had a significant impact on the local economy.*

❦

250 AND 251   **Precocious** versus **Procacious**

ADJECTIVES

Precocious derives from the Latin prefix *prae-*, meaning 'ahead of,' combined with the verb *coquere*, meaning 'to cook'. Originally, the word precocious was a term used in botany to describe early ripening plants. Over time, the word started to be applied to young people of considerable talents beyond their age or experience. Procacious is a rare synonym for impudence or brashness and derives from the Latin *procax*, which has the same meaning but curiously derives from the verb *procare* meaning 'to demand'. Perhaps demanding people are often *procacious*.

He was such a precocious child – piano at six, violin at seven, even his music teacher found it hard to keep up with him!

His procacious remarks caused the Duchess to blush slightly at the young man's brashness.

❧

252 **Maffick**

VERB

A word with a strong historical significance, which was popular in the early decades of the twentieth century but is rarely used nowadays. To maffick is to celebrate something with boisterous abandon. The word derives from the Boer War and the Siege of Mafeking, a battle in which the British Army, although outnumbered, managed to hold firm for 217 days. When news of the lifting of the siege on 17 May 1900 filtered through to Britain, it sparked wild celebrations in towns and cities.

There was much mafficking across Britain to celebrate the Queen's Diamond Jubilee.

❧

253 **Martinet**

NOUN

The term martinet describes a person who is a strict disciplinarian, a hard taskmaster and a stickler for the rules. The word comes from the name of the stern seventeenth-century French soldier, Lieutenant Colonel John Martinet, who served Louis XIV and was famous for his obsessive marshalling of his troops.

I'm so relieved to be rid of my boss. She was such a petty martinet – it was like being in the army!

❧

254 Sardonic

ADJECTIVE

In the ancient world, various writers, including the poet Virgil, mention a poisonous herb found on the island of Sardinia that if ingested caused the facial muscles to go into spasm as if being forced to laugh. The Greek word *sardánios*, meaning 'bitter and scornful laughter', derived from this and in English it was common for writers to mention 'Sardinian laughter' or 'Sardinian smiles'. Sardonic was adopted into English from the French *Sardonique*, originally as *Sardonick*, but by the nineteenth century the capital letter was dropped along with the rather redundant 'k' in the spelling. At this point the relationship of the word to Sardinia was lost but the bitter and scornful meaning still remains.

She shot back a sardonic smile and said: 'Well, I suppose you would, wouldn't you?'

❧

255 Mathesis

NOUN

An archaic word derived from the Greek word *mathēsis*, meaning 'the acquisition of knowledge' or 'the moment of knowing or understanding'. The word is also linked to the modern-day word mathematics, but the Greeks didn't distinguish between the different physical sciences and philosophy, so all knowledge or *mathēsis* was interlinked.

To gain an International Baccalaureate Certificate involves considerable mathesis across a range of academic disciplines.

❦

256 Flounce

VERB

The story behind flounce is an elusive one. The verb's earliest recorded uses in English occurred in the mid-1500s, and some scholars believe it is related to the Scandinavian verb *flunsa*, which in Norwegian means 'to hurry' or 'to walk away briskly' and in Swedish 'to fall with a splash' or 'to plunge'. The connection is uncertain, however, because the *flunsa* verbs did not appear in their respective languages until the eighteenth century, long after flounce surfaced in English. A second distinct sense of flounce, referring to a strip or ruffle of fabric attached on one edge, did not appear in English until the eighteenth century. This version of flounce derives from the Middle English *frouncen*, meaning 'to curl'. The derivation of the modern sense of the verb – meaning to walk away with determination and/or in a state of agitation – is also uncertain but probably relates to the Nordic sense of moving quickly or suddenly. The mystery is how it appeared in English before it appeared in Norwegian, suggesting it may have been a slang term from Old Norse.

Taking offence at his coarse remarks, she flounced out of the room.

❦

257 AND 258   **Assiduous** versus **Assizes**

ADJECTIVE/NOUN

Up until 1972 in England and Wales, assizes were periodical court sessions presided over by a high-ranking judge in regional counties. The assizes were usually convened four times a year to assess the most difficult or complex legal matters, both civil and criminal. Judges presiding over assizes, known as 'justices of assize', were required to be assiduous in the manner in which they assessed the cases brought before them. Not only were their efforts invaluable, but they also serve as a fine demonstration of the etymologies of the words assiduous, assess and assize. All three derive from the Latin verb *assidēre*, which is variously translated as 'to sit beside', 'to take care of' or 'to assist in the office of a judge'. To be assiduous, therefore, means to approach something with great care and attention to detail, to be diligent and preserving. The assizes, meanwhile, were abolished in 1972 by the Courts Act and replaced by the Crown Court system. Assizes is now used occasionally to describe a judicial inquiry presided over by a High Court judge.

> *Although very shy, she was assiduous in her work, displaying a fine attention to detail.*

> *The town, though frequently the centre for medieval assizes and inquisitions, never became a municipal or parliamentary borough.*

∾

259 Scrutinize

VERB

In Latin, *scruta* is the word for rubbish, or the process of sorting out junk and separating what is worthwhile from dross. Originally, the Latin verb *scrutari* meant a formal vote or by extension an examination of votes. The person who is involved in counting votes at an election is called a scrutineer. Over time, the verb scrutinize broadened to mean to look carefully and assiduously (see previous entry) at something, usually to check for errors or wrongdoings.

It's so unfair. I feel I'm being constantly scrutinized.

260 AND 261 Gruntle(d) versus Disgruntle(d)

VERBS/ADJECTIVES

Now here is a curious thing. The word gruntle derives from grunt, the sound animals make, especially pigs. As early as the fourteenth century, gruntle was being used figuratively to describe people moaning or bewailing their lot. In a fake memoir from *circa* 1357 titled *The Travels of John Mandeville*, the eponymous (and wholly fictitious) writer/ explorer describes an encounter with a primitive tribe living near the Garden of Eden who have horns on their heads, are hideous to look at and 'gruntle like swines'. By the seventeenth century, the prefix *dis-* had been added to the common meaning that survives today used to describe someone who is discontented. But wait . . . surely if gruntle had the same meaning previously then disgruntle should mean the opposite? Well, this is a rare case of the prefix 'dis' not acting as a negative but as an intensifier – hence to be disgruntled is to be very gruntled indeed. By the 1920s, however, sharp-eyed wordsmiths began using gruntle and gruntled to mean the opposite of disgruntle, partly as no adequate antonym existed but mostly as a linguistic joke. Eventually, although rarely used in common speech, gruntle has come to be used to mean being made to feel satisfied and in good humour.

> *They were gruntled with a good meal and good conversation.*
>
> W. P. WEBB, *The Great Plains* (1931)
>
> *Samira was very disgruntled by the slow service in the restaurant.*

⁓

262 Bizarre

ADJECTIVE

The origins of the adjective bizarre, meaning strange or odd, are a point of some contention among etymologists. One origin places the word as having derived from the Basque word *bizar*, meaning 'beard'. The story goes that Spanish Castilian soldiers had long beards and during many skirmishes with the Basques (who were clean-shaven and had a general antipathy to facial hair) on the foothills of the Pyrenees, the local soldiers refered to the enemy as *bizars* on account of their pointy beards (which presumably they found bizarre). Despite being a humorous story, it is disputed by some scholars who point to the Italian Latin word *bizzarro* from *bizza*, meaning a tendency to be irascible or have quick and unpredictable flashes of temper. By the sixteenth century, the word had migrated into French to mean odd and eccentric and eventually in English to mean strange and weird. It was originally used to describe people's behaviour and characteristics but is used more generally now to describe anything out of the ordinary – which in a sense is how the Basques were using it when confronted by bearded Spaniards.

> *My neighbour's antics have become increasingly bizarre: I looked out of the window yesterday and he was hopping around his garden stark naked, flapping his arms like a bird.*

❧

263, 264 AND 265 **Recidivism** versus **Deciduous** versus **Incident**

NOUN/ADJECTIVE/NOUN

Recidivism derives from the Latin word *recidivus*, meaning 'something recurring'. Recidivists are people who have a tendency to relapse into old habits and the word is often used in legal language to denote persistent criminal offenders. Deciduous and incident are two other English words that have their roots in the Latin verb *cadere* meaning 'to fall'. Deciduous derives from the verb *decidere* (*de-* plus *cadere*), meaning 'to fall off', and is used mainly in botany and horticulture to describe trees and shrubs that shed their leaves or drop their mature fruit. It is occasionally applied to mammals that shed their teeth or snakes and lizards that shed their skin. Incident derives from *incidere* (*in-* plus *cadere*), which means to fall into something, such as an unwanted or unforeseen situation.

> *The judge, when passing sentence, made pointed reference to the accused's recidivism after being previously released from prison.*

The line of deciduous trees along the edge of the lake looked stunning in autumn.

An incident took place yesterday on the main street and traffic is still not being allowed through.

❧

266 Lewd

ADJECTIVE

Another word with a somewhat murky origin and one with various meanings that have evolved over time. It is thought that the origins of the word date back to the Old English word *lǣwede*, meaning 'layman', and was coined to distinguish the laity from the clergy. Given that the clergy were educated and most of the laity were not, over time the word took on the meaning of being stupid or ignorant. By the Middle English period, however, lewd had begun to take on its contemporary meaning of lascivious, obscene and vulgar, as evidenced by Chaucer using the word in this sense in the prologue to *The Miller's Tale*:

> *Lat be thy lewed dronken harlotrye.*
> *It is a sinne and eek a greet folye*
> *To apeiren any man, or him diffame,*
> *And eek to bringen wyves in swich fame*

> *(Stop your drunken talk about sex!*
> *It's a sin and bad form*
> *to hurt another man's reputation with such stories,*
> *especially when you drag their wives into it too.)*

Geoffrey Chaucer, *The Canterbury Tales* (1476)

❧

267 AND 268 Sedulous versus Sedentary

ADJECTIVES

Sedulous derives from the Latin *se dolus,* which means 'without guile'. The modern notion of guile is having a sharp skill or quick wits, but in the Middle Ages someone with guile was not to be trusted as they would most likely cheat you or trick you. The word sedulous is not related to words such as 'sedentary' or 'sedate' (which derive from the Latin verb *sedēre,* meaning 'to sit'). Sedulous people are not the sedate or sedentary sort, they are go-getters who set about things with care and diligence. English speakers borrowed sedentary in the late sixteenth century from Middle French *sedentaire*, which in turn derives from the Latin *sedentarius. Sedentarius*, which means 'of one that sits', is from the present participle of the verb *sedēre*, meaning 'to sit'.

> *She set about the decorating with sedulous attention to detail.*

> *I have a sedentary office job and have to get up from my desk to stretch my legs several times a day.*

269 Insidious

ADJECTIVE

Insidious is a nasty word which derived from the Latin *insidiae*, meaning 'to ambush'. This sense of something being imperceptibly harmful can be applied to both people and situations and carries the implication of furtiveness and deceit, such as an insidious conspiracy to topple a government or leader. Insidious is also sometimes applied to the slow development of certain debilitating diseases, such as 'insidious cancers'.

*The insidious whispers that surrounded her
every time she walked into the office gradually
wore her down.*

❧

270 Sedens

NOUN

A rare word, closely linked in meaning to sedentary as it also
derives from the Latin *sedēre* meaning 'to sit'. Sedens is most
commonly used to describe people who live the whole of
their life either in or very close to their place of birth.

*The philosopher Emanuel Kant was a renowned
sedens, he never lived or travelled further than ten
miles from his family home.*

❧

271 Macrosomatic

ADJECTIVE

A term in zoology to describe animals, mostly mammals,
with enhanced olfactory senses – that is primarily, the
sense of smell. Dogs have a keen sense of smell, which has
developed largely for hunting purposes. There are several
myths about supposedly macrosomatic animals, one being
that elephants can smell water from miles away and that
sharks can smell droplets of blood in the sea from similar
distances. This later myth was given credence by the film
Jaws (1977), when in fact there is no proof that sharks can
smell blood from any further than a few hundred yards.

*My dog is macrosomatic; all I have to do is open
the fridge and he comes bounding into the kitchen
expecting to be fed.*

272 Impignorate

VERB

You know that things are getting desperate if you are forced to impignorate. Derived from the Latin *pignerare*, meaning 'to pledge', impignorate is an old-fashioned word for pawning or mortgaging possessions in order to gain money, with a pledge to pay the received sum back. Scottish writer Robert Louis Stevenson (1850–1894) was particularly fond of the word and used it several times to describe moments of hardship during his voyages across the South Seas exploring Pacific islands.

> *Austerity measures and rising prices are forcing people to impignorate anything they own of value in order to make ends meet.*

273 Ignoscible

ADJECTIVE

Have you ever been in a situation where a friend has done something stupid, yet you know there were mitigating circumstances? Well, then, you were in an ignoscible position. Derived from the Latin *ignoscibilis* meaning 'to pardon' or literally 'not to wish to know', ignoscible is a great word, the obscurity of which sums up those awkward feelings we'd rather forget or not think too deeply about. Sometimes, it is best not to know in ignoscible situations.

> *My grandfather suffered from dementia; and late in life he would scream out obscenities or start telling lewd stories at the dinner table. I found the whole situation ignoscible and it made me sad.*

274   Supervacaneous

ADJECTIVE

A rare adjective that is more or less a synonym of superfluous. If there is any difference between the two words, other than supervacaneous is hardly used, it could possibly be that something superfluous is an excess in some form before something occurs – as in 'superfluous to requirements'. Supervacaneous, however, is when the surplus/needless waste is realized afterwards, usually through an error or oversight. They can be used interchangeably but almost nobody will know what you are saying if you use supervacaneous – so try it!

> *The orders for the wedding were all wrong – there were supervacaneous crates of beer left over the next day.*

275 AND 276   Misconstrue versus Misunderstand

VERBS

To construe, in the old-fashioned sense, is to analyse the meaning and syntax of a sentence. It has its root in the Latin *construere*, meaning 'construction'. In the fifteenth century, English speakers adopted construe to mean interpreting words constructed in a sentence and added the prefix *mis-*, meaning wrong. It is often assumed that misconstrue and misunderstand are interchangeable and in some contexts they are, but there are fine differences in usage. At a base level, to misunderstand something is to get something wrong; it is a largely inadvertent and an unfortunate occurrence usually due to a breakdown in communication. To misconstrue is to misinterpret something said or done and draw erroneous conclusions. Misconstrue is a far more active process; most misunderstandings happen by accident.

> *He misconstrued my offer of a drink to mean I was giving him a come on.*

> *I'm so sorry – I misunderstood the directions you gave me, which is why I was late.*

❧

277 **Gormless**

ADJECTIVE

The origins of gormless derive from an amalgamation of the dialect noun *gaum,* meaning 'attention' or 'understanding', and the suffix *–less*. In Old English, to have gaum meant that a person was quite sharp-witted. This word however completely vanished, possibly because people realized there were more stupid people in the world than clever ones. Thus the meaning of gormless is to have little or no capacity for understanding or paying attention. There is also the verb 'to gaum', which derived from Celtic dialects and meant 'to pay attention', but this has become virtually obsolete. Gormless continues to be widely used to describe people who are not quite with it.

> *The new intern hasn't a clue; he walks around the office with a perpetual gormless expression on his face.*

❧

278 Dismal

ADJECTIVE

In the Middle Ages, alongside saints' days and holy festivals, the calendar was also marked with what was known as 'Egyptian days'. These days were regarded as inauspicious, probably as a relic of ancient Egyptian belief, and treated with superstition akin to the thirteenth day of the month falling on a Friday. Many medieval writers, including Chaucer, interpreted them to be anniversaries of the Biblical plagues in Egypt. There were twenty-four such days per year, and in Anglo-French they were called collectively dismal (from Latin *dies mali*, 'evil days'), and this word was borrowed into Middle English. In time, the 'evil days' sense was forgotten and dismal was simply taken to mean 'disastrous'. By the mid-twentieth century, however, dismal had taken on a far less sinister and foreboding meaning and is generally applied to anything pretty bad, pathetic and lamentable.

> *The team's record away from home has been pretty dismal for several seasons.*

❧

279 Sycophant

NOUN

In ancient Greece if you bad-mouthed someone you were a *sykophantēs*, a slanderer. The origins of the word are unclear, due in part to the first part of the word deriving from the Greek word for a fig (*sykon*). Since the sixteenth century, there has been a theory that the term related to the taxes Greek farmers were required to pay on the figs they transported to market or exported. Some farmers would attempt to evade making the payments to the civil authorities, who retaliated by paying informants to pass on information about any tax dodgers. There are, however, no historical texts that support this idea. Latin originally kept the 'slanderer' sense, however, when the word migrated to English it developed a sense of someone creeping up to a person in a position of influence for personal gain.

> *I don't trust him – he's a sycophant, always creeping up to the boss.*

280 Augur

VERB

In ancient Rome the *augurs* were official soothsayers whose purpose was not to predict the future, but to decide if a certain action or situation met with the approval of the gods. The *augurs* used various methods to draw their conclusions, such as observing natural phenomenon like the weather or the flight of birds, or scrutinizing the innards of dead animals. When the verb was adopted into English it retained this sense of looking for promising or reassuring signs in something and it is often used with an adverb, such as 'well'.

> *The bright weather forecast augurs well for the holiday weekend.*

281 Oleaginous

ADJECTIVE

We have all met slippery, furtive people, either personally or professionally, that we may describe as oily. The elegant adjective oleaginous expresses this less-than-attractive character trait perfectly. The Latin word *oleaginous* meant 'from an olive tree'. Archaeological evidence suggests olives were being farmed and processed into olive oil as early as 4000 BC, so *oleaginous* was at first used in a literal sense (meaning made from olives), which is still permissible today if, for example, describing a particularly oily salad dressing. By the nineteenth century, oleaginous had developed its contemporary meaning of somebody who has an offensively ingratiating manner.

> *The scent, the smile but more than these, the dark*
> *eyes and oleaginous address brought home at*
> *duskfall many a commission to the head of the firm*
> *seated with Jacob's pipe after like labours in the*
> *paternal ingle (a meal of noodles, you may be sure, is*
> *aheating), reading through round horned spectacles*
> *some paper from the Europe of a month before.*

JAMES JOYCE, *Ulysses* (1922)

꙳

282 Pandemonium

NOUN

The word pandemonium is used to describe any chaotic or seemingly lawless situation. We have the poet John Milton (1608–1674) to thank for first coining the phrase. In Milton's *Paradise Lost*, Pandaemonium is the capital of hell where Satan reigns with his council of evil spirits. Milton formed the word by combining the Greek words *pan* meaning 'all' and *daimónion* meaning 'evil spirits' – hence it is the place where all evil spirits reside. The contemporary sense of a chaotic commotion developed in the nineteenth century.

> *A solemn Council forthwith to be held*
> *At Pandaemonium, the high Capital*
> *Of Satan and his Peers*

JOHN MILTON, *Paradise Lost*, Book One (1667)

283 Lampoon

NOUN/VERB

Lampoon can function as a noun or a verb. To lampoon is to satirise a person or thing for comedic effect and arrived in English in the seventeenth century. The word originated from the French word *lampon,* meaning 'to gulp down or guzzle'. *Lampons!* Or 'let us guzzle!' is a common chorus in seventeenth-century French satirical folk poems and humorous drinking songs. One assumes the targets of these bawdy, scathing ditties were well and truly lampooned.

> *The actor didn't take kindly to being lampooned on* Saturday Night Live *and took to Twitter to voice his annoyance.*

284 Boilerplate

NOUN/ADJECTIVE

Boilerplate text, or simply boilerplate, is any written text that can be reused in new contexts or applications without significant changes to the original. In the days before computers, small, local newspapers relied heavily on feature stories, editorials and other printed material supplied by large publishing consortiums. The syndicates delivered the material on metal plates with the type already in place so the local papers wouldn't have to set it. Printers apparently dubbed those syndicated plates boiler plates because of their resemblance to the plating used in making steam boilers. Soon boilerplate came to refer to the printed material on the plates as well as to the plates themselves. Because boilerplate stories were more often filler than hard news, the word acquired negative connotations and became an adjective to describe hackneyed or unoriginal writing.

> *The author's agent wanted to establish a boilerplate contract with the publisher – it would save time in the long run.*

❧

285 Oxymoron

NOUN

In the great centres of education in Ancient Greece, such as Plato's Academy and Aristotle's Lyceum, the study of rhetoric was taken very seriously. To this end, the Greeks systematically categorized the elements of rhetoric required to speak, write and (most importantly) argue effectively and persuasively. The word is derived from *oxys* meaning 'sharp' and *moros,* meaning 'foolish' (also the root stem for the insult, moron). Oxymoron originally had positive connotations and described expressive paradoxes in short elegant phrases that were seemingly self-contradictory. Poets were particularly fond of using oxymorons as a literary device, as in Juliet's famous line in the balcony scene of *Romeo and Juliet* (see below). However, over time the word has developed an often negative connotation when applied to muddled expressions or unintentional contradictions. Interestingly, oxymorons surface in figures of speech in day-to-day language and nobody bats an eyelid when someone gives an 'unbiased opinion' on something 'awfully good'.

> *Parting is such sweet sorrow,*
> *That I shall say good night till it be morrow.*
>
> WILLIAM SHAKESPEARE, *Romeo and Juliet*, Act 2, Scene 2 (*c.* 1595)

286 Intoxicate

VERB

A somewhat confused word that is increasingly used in both positive and negative senses. Intoxicate derives from *toxicum*, the Latin word for poison, and the initial meaning of the verb was to poison someone or something. Its common usage is to describe somebody who has lost control of their physical and mental faculties through excessive intake of alcohol and drugs. Usually the implication is that the intoxication has been self-inflicted but the meaning is retained if a person has unwittingly been poisoned. However, from the mid-twentieth century, the word began to be used figuratively by writers to describe becoming excited or overcome with sensual elation. This is rather silly when you think about it: 'He was intoxicated by the smell of her perfume.' Really? He was poisoned by the smell of her perfume? Best not stand too close to her then.

> *After a whole day of drinking in the sunshine, he was thoroughly intoxicated and needed to be helped home.*

287 Gerrymander

VERB

Former vice-president of the United States Elbridge Gerry (1744–1814) was a slippery operator. When, in 1811, Gerry was re-elected as governor of Massachusetts, he promptly set about redrawing the state's district boundaries so as to give his party, the Democrats, a huge majority of seats in the state senate (at the expense of the Federalist opposition). Legend has it that Benjamin Russell, the editor of a Federalist-supporting newspaper, *The Columbian Centinel*, was in his office scratching his head over a map of the proposed boundary changes when his friend, the portrait artist Gilbert Stuart, entered the room. Stuart is said to have taken the map and doctored it by adding a head and claws of a lizard and said: 'There you go – a salamander.'

'More like a Gerrymander,' was Russell's retort. Despite widespread protests, Gerry got his own way and was able to push a bill through the senate effecting the changes. The term has since passed into political vernacular to describe any attempt to rig a vote by altering existing sizes of districts or constituencies in order to gain an unfair advantage.

> *Successive governments have used the boundary commission to effectively gerrymander subsequent elections in the sitting party's favour.*

288 Blackguard

NOUN

> *Shall a gentleman so well descended as Camillo – a lousy slave that within this twenty years rode with the black guards in the Duke's carriage, 'mongst spits and dripping-pans.*

JOHN WEBSTER, *The White Devil*, Act 1 (1612)

So speaks the scheming Flamineo in John Webster's baroque renaissance tragedy *The White Devil*. Flamineo is questioning the background of his brother-in-law by suggesting that he was once a black guard – a lowly servant. Originally, black guards worked in the kitchens of aristocratic families in the Middle Ages. It was hot and grimy work tending to the blackened pots and the furnace-like ovens. By the eighteenth century, the word appears in Francis Grose's *Dictionary of the Vulgar Tongue* with the definition: 'dirty tattered and roguish boys'. Black guards had then turned from downtrodden servants to street urchins and eventually became rogues and thieves.

> *I find the hypocrisy around state visits by dubious dictators hard to take as the government has long welcomed blackguards and thieves.*

289 and 290   **Eponymous** and **Eponym**

ADJECTIVE/NOUN

Eponymous derives from the Greek adjective *eponymous* ('having a significant name'), which in turn derives from *onyma,* meaning 'name'. *Onyma* has provided the root to a number of other English words, including synonymous, pseudonym and anonymous. Traditionally, an eponymous person or thing (i.e., an eponym) might be a mythical ancestor or totem believed to be the source of a clan's name. In modern usage, eponymous typically refers to the person who gives their name to something – such as the eponymous heroine of *Bridget Jones' Diary*. Often, the capital letter is dropped to lower case when a name is used to stand in for a noun, as has happened with products such as aspirin, biro and diesel – the latter two are actually proprietary products as they take their names from the

Hungarian inventor László Bíró and German scientist
Rudolf Diesel respectively.

> *Many critics believe The Smiths' eponymous first
> album to be their best.*

> *The verb to hoover the carpet is said regularly by
> people regardless of which brand of vacuum cleaner
> they are using; it is an example of an eponym.*

∽

291 Insuperable

ADJECTIVE

Insuperable is a near synonym of insurmountable and
derives from the Latin *superare*, meaning 'to go over' or
overcome. The addition of the negative prefix *in-* with
superare plus *abilis,* the Latin for able, forms *insuperabilis*,
meaning 'something that cannot be overcome or
surmounted'. The word can describe physical barriers that
cannot be scaled (such as walls or mountains) as well as
more figurative challenges, obstacles or difficulties.

> *Shackleton encountered seemingly insuperable
> problems during his voyages to the Antarctic but
> miraculously survived.*

∽

292 Toady

NOUN

The term toady has its roots in the travelling entertainers
and showmen of seventeenth-century Europe. One
common spectacle at county fetes and fayres was for a
'miracle worker' to put on a show, often to illustrate their

healing powers in order to sell quack medicines. One such act involved a showman's assistant swallowing a live toad and then regurgitating it. Toads were commonly thought to be poisonous but actually weren't as toxic as was assumed. The toadeater would swallow the toad and collapse in agony only for the showman to revive them and 'cure' them by some means. This con trick led to the word toadeater becoming synonymous with a servant or underling willing to go to any lengths in the service of a master and over time was shortened to toady.

> *You won't get very far if you insist on toadying to the second-in-command!*

~~~

293　Flabbergast

VERB

The origins of flabbergast are unclear but it is first recorded in English in 1772. One theory is that it was a dialectal term that entered into common usage from fashionable society. There was a great interest in word coinage around this time as evidenced by the huge popularity of Doctor Johnson's dictionary, so it is highly possible that the word is a concoction of 'flabby' and 'aghast' to describe being dumbstruck in open-mouthed astonishment. Aghast traces back to a Middle English verb, *gasten,* meaning 'to frighten'. *Gasten* (which also provides the root stem for *ghastly,* meaning terrible or frightening) comes from *gast*, a Middle English spelling of the word ghost. People who were flabbergasted then had the appearance – originally at least – of someone who had just seen a ghost.

> *Joe was flabbergasted by the amount of mess his teenage son managed to make every day.*

294   Tantalize

VERB

In Greek mythology, King Tantalus of Phrygia offended
the ancient gods by stealing food from Zeus's table and
betraying their secrets. As punishment, Tantalus was
plunged up to his chin in chains in the waters of Hades,
where he had to stand beneath overhanging boughs of a
tree heavily laden with ripe, juicy fruit. Although he was
continually hungry and thirsty, Tantalus could neither
drink the water nor eat the fruit, as every time he reached
for them, the fruit would sway away from his grasp and
the water would recede. The word tantalize came into
English in the sixteenth century when stories of the myths
of antiquity were hugely popular, including the tale of
hapless Tantalus. The nineteenth century saw the creation
of the Tantalus cup (also known as the Pythagorean cup)
– a novelty trick cup with a secret syphoning device that
drains itself when filled up to a certain point. Tantalize
is used generally as a word to describe teasing and
tormenting by presenting something desirable in view but
continually keeping it agonizingly out of reach.

> *The Disney Corporation have been tantalizing* Star
> Wars *fans with slow-drip leaks of mini-trailers for
> the blockbuster sequels.*

❧

295   Agastopia

NOUN

A curious word given to a rare and not very well
documented mental health issue. Agastopia is an all-
consuming love for a particular part of another person's
body. It isn't just wishing you had a six-pack and abs like

your neighbour who goes to the gym every day – it is much weirder than that and can occasionally become a dangerous obsession.

Is having a foot fetish a form of agastopia, or just a bit kinky?

❧

296 **Gabelle**

NOUN

In France, the *gabelle* was a very unpopular tax on salt that was established during the mid-fourteenth century and lasted, with brief lapses and revisions, up until the end of the Second World War. The term gabelle is derived from the Italian *gabella*, meaning 'a duty'. Gabelle is often used as a rather fancy way of describing some particularly unfair stealth tax or duty or hidden charge, such as booking fees on concert tickets for which there seems little or no justification.

The hotel's insistence that we pay extra to use the safety deposit box in our room was clearly just a gabelle.

❧

297 **Lamprophony**

NOUN

Lamprophony means loud and clear annunciation – it is not a word to apply to mumblers. The word derives from the ancient Greek *lampró*, meaning 'loud and clear', and *phōnos*, the word for sound. Arguably, any animal that makes loud and clear sounds could feasibly be described as lamprophonic.

We were awoken every morning by the lamprophony of the cawing gulls at daybreak.

∽

298 Xertz

VERB

It's pretty common practice for impatient readers to skip the introduction or preface of a book and dive straight in. I'm guilty of it myself. However, the definition of this word and its origin are discussed in the introduction so if you didn't bother reading it – or weren't paying attention – check it out (again?).

Come on – let's xertz these drinks and get on the dancefloor!

∽

299 Philodox

NOUN

A philodox is a person much enamoured with their own opinions and thoughts. The word is derived from the Ancient Greek *philódoxos*, meaning 'opinion-loving'. It is nice to be right, or better still try to be right, but to be a philodox is the wrong way about achieving rightness.

I really can't abide my father-in-law; he is a philodox. It doesn't matter what the discussion is about, he has an opinion even if he knows nothing about the subject.

∽

300 Flapdoodle

NOUN

Flapdoodle, alongside its close relatives folderol and fiddle-faddle, is of unknown origin. The word first appeared towards the end of the nineteenth century and simply means nonsense. The Victorians were rather fond of inventing words that mean nothing at all, as evidenced in the works of Edward Lear and Lewis Carroll.

> *Well, Oscar, that last poem of yours is a load of old flapdoodle.*

---

301 Lackadaisical

ADJECTIVE

'Alack the day, she's dead, she's dead, she's dead,' wails Lady Capulet on discovering Juliet's body (*Romeo and Juliet*, Act 4, Scene 5). Juliet isn't actually dead at this point (although soon will be) but in a self-induced coma. 'Alack the day' was a common expression of sorrow and disappointment in the sixteenth century and means simply 'curse the day'. It was most commonly used for days when nothing seems to go right or on 'dismal' days (see page 139). By the seventeenth century, this colloquial phrase had been condensed into 'lackaday', which had more or less the same meaning. By the eighteenth century, the expression had developed into the adjective lackadaisical, which initially denoted the limp and downbeat demeanour of someone having a truly bad day. In modern usage it has developed a subsidiary meaning of sluggishness – as if things aren't really worth bothering with when everything will go wrong anyhow.

His recent lackadaisical approach to work had led his colleagues to feel he had slipped back into depression.

❧

302 AND 303 **Demeanour** versus **Demean**

ADJECTIVE/VERB

Despite the closeness of their spellings (a fact that must bemuse learners of English as a foreign language), these two words derive from different roots. There is a long journey through the Latin origins of demeanour before arriving at the modern English word, meaning 'outward manner' and 'behaviour towards others'. The trail starts with the Latin verb *minari*, meaning 'to threaten', and *minare*, a word once specifically used to describe the herding of cattle and the shouts (presumably threatening) of cattle drivers. The word then moved into Anglo-French and the verb *mener*, 'to lead', and then *demener,* 'to conduct'. From this derives the Middle English *demenen*, a close relative of the modern English demean, both meaning 'to conduct (oneself) in a certain manner'. Finally, add the suffix *-our* to demean and we arrive at demeanour. It is uncertain if the suffix was added to distinguish it from the verb demean, which arrived in English via a very different root. To demean someone (or oneself) is to degrade and to be lowered to a base level. The word derives from the Middle English *mene*, which meant 'lowly and common', which in turn derived from the Old English word or Germanic origins *ġemǽne*, meaning 'mean and base'.

> *I could tell she was nervous on her first date by her demeanour, as she kept fiddling with her hair and glancing at her cell phone.*
>
> *I could never work for a fast food chain as I would find the experience very demeaning.*

304   Kummerspeck

NOUN

A German word that has gained some currency (or should that be weight?) in English in the twenty-first century, largely in media circles and on the internet. The word is a compound of *kummer*, meaning grief, and *speck*, which can mean either bacon or lard/fat. The closest literal translation therefore is 'grief bacon', which sounds amusing but is actually no laughing matter. Kummerspeck is sudden gaining of weight through excessive comfort eating, due to grief or low spirits.

> *I gained considerable kummerspeck after I split up with my ex; I was getting through a tub of ice cream after every meal.*

305   Dysania

NOUN

Another modern depression-related word, dysania is a mental condition whereby a person finds it very difficult to get out of bed in the mornings. This is often a symptom of severe stress and anxiety and/or the result of sleep deprivation. It is also sometimes referred to in medical journals as clinomania, and although rare can become very debilitating.

> *I'm sorry I was late for work this morning; I suffer from terrible dysania.*

306 Enamour

VERB

To enamour is to captivate with love or inspire admiration and respect. It is not surprising therefore that the word has its roots in the French word for love, *amour* (Latin *amor*). Since the mid-twentieth century, the adjectival form 'enamoured' has regularly been used in negative form, almost as a polite understatement.

> *She was far from enamoured with the arduous train journey she had to endure every morning.*

307 Accoutrement

NOUN

Derived from the Middle French verb *accoutre* (to outfit or provide with equipment), accoutrement originally referred to personal items soldiers carried with them in their kit bags. In modern parlance, accoutrements are often regarded as fashionable items – accessories such as hats, gloves, handbags and jewellery. Quite where the connection between the military and high fashion was formed is anybody's guess, except perhaps for the fact that French soldiers were generally well dressed and conscious of their appearance.

> *When entering the departure lounges at any major airport, one becomes swamped by hundreds of duty-free shops selling all manner of high-end fashion accoutrements.*

308 AND 309 **Omnipotent** versus **Omniscient**

ADJECTIVES

Omnipotent and omniscient originally referred specifically to the power held by an almighty God. Both words are formed with the prefix *omni-*, meaning 'all' in Latin, and then either *potens* – meaning potent or powerful (hence all-powerful) – or *sciens*, meaning knowledge. If one is omniscient it means one has infinite knowledge, awareness, understanding, insight or perception.

> *The belief in an omnipotent and omniscient god sits at the bedrock of most religious faiths.*

310 **Tonsorial**

ADJECTIVE

Tonsorial has the broad meaning of pertaining or relating to the work done by barbers and hairdressers. In Latin, the verb *tondēre* had the meaning of 'to shear' something. Historically, the related word *tonsure* described the practice of cutting and shaving the scalp of the head as part of religious rites, such as the bald scalps traditionally sported by Catholic monks (although this practice has now been abolished).

> *She honed her tonsorial skills at a top Paris hair salon before setting up her own business.*

311 Apology

NOUN

As children we are taught from an early age to say sorry when we have done something wrong – that is, to make an apology. The common modern usage of apology is a spoken or written admission of error or discourtesy, accompanied usually by an expression of regret. However, originally apology meant something very different. Apology derives from the Greek/Latin word *apologia* meaning 'a speech given in one's defence', and so when people made an apology they weren't saying sorry at all; on the contrary, they were seeking justification for their words and deeds. By the late sixteenth century, however, apology came to mean an explanation for something and eventually an admission of culpability – the meaning that is prevalent to this day. So next time someone proffers an apology, it is worth considering from a semantic point of view whether they are really filled with remorse or merely justifying their actions!

> *I asked for a full and frank apology but all I received were some flimsy excuses.*

312 Atone

VERB

While on the subject of the insincerity of offering apologies, let's have a look at another sorry verb. In Middle English the word *aton* had the meaning of being 'at one' with the world and of being in harmony. Originally, the verb atone had the implication of seeking a reconciliation or restoring harmony between two factions, people or groups. In modern usage, atone is usually used in the sense of making amends for some error or misjudgement usually by way of apology or reparation.

> *The goalkeeper atoned for his early errors by saving two penalties during the shootout.*

❧

313 AND 314 **Excruciate** versus **Excruciating**

VERB/ADJECTIVE

Excruciate is a verb that is almost always used with an object. Derived from the Latin *excruciāre*, meaning 'to torment or torture', to excruciate someone was basically to inflict severe physical and/or mental pain upon someone. *Excruciāre* also has links with 'to crucify' – which makes sense as being nailed to a cross and left to slowly asphyxiate must have been an excruciatingly painful method of execution. This is worth remembering as the adjective excruciating is often used hyperbolically to describe awkward social situations: migraines are excruciatingly painful; your dad dancing at a wedding is just something you find mildly embarrassing.

> *The despot rules by fear, deploying various methods to excruciate his enemies by inflicting almost medieval atrocities.*
>
> *The best man's speech was excruciating. Clearly drunk, he made several inappropriate jokes about the bride's former boyfriends.*

❧

315   Unwieldy

ADJECTIVE

The definition of the verb to wield is 'to handle or apply something effectively'. An experienced lumberjack is no doubt skilful with an axe, for example, or a gifted public speaker could wield significant power over their audience. Curiously, the verb to wield isn't commonly used, often being resigned to the tools used in physical labour. Something that is unwieldly is much more prevalent and can be applied to anything that is difficult to handle physically. Both wield and its antonym derive from the Old English *wieldan,* meaning 'to control', which itself derived from the Proto-Germanic word *walth*, meaning 'to have power' over something.

> *My grandfather's petrol lawnmower is very unwieldy; he really should buy a new one.*

316   Gingerly

ADJECTIVE/ADVERB

There is much debate among etymologists as to the exact origin of the adjective/adverb gingerly. One theory is that it derives from the Old French word *gensor*, meaning 'delicate' and 'slight'. This theory has partial corroboration with the root of that word, again from Old French, *gent*, one of the meanings of which was to be graceful and elegant in repose. Suddenly, however, by the seventeenth century the word gingerly had taken on a much more cautious meaning. To proceed with an action gingerly wasn't to do something with a graceful flourish but to be reticent and almost reluctant.

> *He descended the ladder gingerly, mindful of slipping and injuring himself.*

317 **Matelot**

NOUN

A matelot is an old-fashioned word for a sailor. The word derives from the Dutch word *mattenoot*, meaning bedmate, and came into English via Middle French. The origins of the word reside in the practice of sailors sharing hammocks in the sleeping quarters.

> *The matelot took us out to sea in a decidedly dodgy-looking boat.*

318 **Puckish**

ADJECTIVE

Puck is best known in English as 'that merry wanderer of the night' in William Shakespeare's *A Midsummer Night's Dream* (Act 2, Scene 1). One of Shakespeare's most colourful characters, the mischief-making servant of King Oberon certainly knew how to sow merry hell and mayhem. In Medieval English folklore, however, Puck was an altogether more unpleasant and dangerous spirit: a devil-like goblin known as puke or pouke, names closely related to the Old Norse *pūki,* meaning devil, is the likely source for Shakespeare's lovable rogue. However, the adjective puckish relates directly to Shakespeare's creation and means mischievous but not necessarily truly evil.

> *In the film* The Mask, *Jim Carrey's character indulges in all manner of puckish antics in the role of his eponymous anti-hero.*

319 Indwell

VERB

Indwell is an archaic verb that hails from the fourteenth century when there were common beliefs around spirits, both good and evil, that acted as forces upon human life by indwelling the soul. The word is thought to have been first coined by the theologian John Wycliffe (1320s–84) in his groundbreaking Bible translations and philosophical writings. Ironically, following his death, Wycliffe was renounced as a heretic for being spiritually bereft and his corpse was exhumed from consecrated ground and burned.

> *Open your soul and let the power and love of God indwell.*

320 AND 321 Inimical versus Inimitable

ADJECTIVES

It is a common error to confuse these two words, as they sound very alike, but they mean radically different things. Inimical derives from the Latin word for enemy – *inimicus*. Inimical forces are malevolent and hostile and wish to do harm. Inimitable, on the other hand, means something that can't be copied or imitated, like the inimitable guitar-playing of Jimi Hendrix or the unique footballing prowess of Lionel Messi.

> *She flashed him a hard, inimical stare.*

> *It was a stellar performance delivered in the group's own inimitable style.*

322 **Jugulate**

VERB

A rather nasty term, of medical origin (usually used in autopsy reports), to jugulate is to slit somebody's throat.

The Colombian drug gangs' favourite form of retribution is to jugulate their victims, hang them upside down and watch them bleed to death.

323 **Cancel**

VERB

In ancient Rome, when a legal document was nullified it was crossed through with vertical and horizontal lines to create a lattice pattern. The word comes from a Latin noun, *cancelli*, meaning 'lattice', and originally referred to these crosshatched lines drawn to signify what was deleted. Towards the end of the fifteenth century, the word developed its general sense of not only crossing something out but cancelling anything from debts to appointments and public events.

I've tried several times to cancel my subscription online, yet they still keep taking money from my bank account.

324 **Jargon**

NOUN

It is not uncommon to hear of 'jargon-busting' in modern life – laudable attempts to cut through the proliferation of meta-language attached to a particular subject. In medieval times the word jargon was borrowed into English from Anglo-French *jargoun*, which related to birdsong and in particular the chirping and chattering of sparrows and starlings. However, by the fourteenth century, jargon started to be applied to garrulous people. Chaucer describes the knight January as being somewhat full of himself and chattering like a magpie in *The Merchant's Tale*: 'He was al coltissh ful of ragerye, And ful of iargon as a flekked pie.' Over the next two centuries, jargon developed a more generalized meaning of any words, symbols or signs that were meaningless or difficult to understand. In modern usage, jargon tends to be used either for specialized language related to a particular field – such as computer technology – or, rather negatively, reflecting its original sense, of meaningless or superfluous prattle.

> *I tried reading the instruction manual but got bogged down in all the jargon.*

❧

325 Haggard

ADJECTIVE

The art of falconry is the sport of hunting with trained birds of prey such as a kestrel or peregrine falcon. Customarily, falconers trained wild birds by taking them from their nests when younglings or capturing them as young adult birds. The older the bird is when it is captured the harder it is to tame and these birds were known as haggards. In the seventeenth century, the falconry sense of *haggard* began to be used in a more descriptive way and was applied to someone wild, stubborn and obdurate like a captured bird. Shakespeare's Petruchio uses this metaphor when describing his protracted 'taming' of Katherine. By the nineteenth century, the word came to express the way the human face looks when a person is drained, fretful or shocked, as no doubt the captured birds of prey were in days of yore. In contemporary usage, haggard retains this sense of being tired and gaunt.

> *Another way I have to man my haggard,*
> *To make her come and know her keeper's call;*
> *That is to watch her as we watch those kites*
> *That bate, and beat, and will not be obedient.*

> WILLIAM SHAKESPEARE, *The Taming of the Shrew*,
> Act 4, Scene 1 (*c.* 1590)

326 Deracinate

VERB

The word deracinate entered English from the Middle French word *desraciner* meaning 'to uproot'. Originally, the word referred simply to pulling up plants by the root. Over time, however, deracinate developed a metaphorical meaning relating to removing cultural and ethical influences from people or groups.

> *One major problem working-class students encounter at elite universities is a sense of being deracinated from their background.*

327 Eavesdrop

VERB

The eaves of a building are the overhanging parts of the roof that cover the external walls. Therefore the eaves' drops are the drips of rainwater dropping from the roof onto the ground below. In one of many creative uses of the English language a rather dull effect of the weather became a verb describing the activity of listening in on other people's conversations – presumably, in a figurative sense, catching drips and drops of information.

> *Shakespeare's plays, especially the comedies, are marred by the repetitive use of eavesdropping as a plot device.*

❦

328 Fiasco

NOUN

Audiences at La Scala opera house in Milan are notoriously discriminating; one false note is enough to have the audience erupt into a cacophony of boos and hisses. The great Maria Callas suffered the indignity of being showered with carrots and cabbages during a performance of *Medea* in the 1960s because she wobbled slightly during one of the arias; the projectiles were no doubt accompanied by the traditional disparaging cry of '*Ola! Ola! Fiasco!*' The word fiasco, meaning a disaster or debacle, has its roots in the Italian word for a bottle or flask, from the Latin word *flasco*. The sense of fiasco meaning an embarrassing failure derived from the Italian idiomatic expression *fare fiasco*, which literally translates as 'to make a bottle' – to fail. Quite where the etymological connection between bottle-making and failure derives from is a matter of some conjecture, although one theory is that skilled glassblowers recycled defective crystalware into ordinary bottles if they were found to have imperfections.

> *She turned what was otherwise a truly memorable event into a fiasco that will be remembered for all the wrong reasons!*

329 **Curfew**

NOUN

In the Middle Ages, most houses in towns and villages across Europe were built of wood. Commonly, particularly in towns, the houses were built dangerously close to the house next door. Unsurprisingly, as all dwellings had open fires, an untended hearth could spread flames rapidly across local houses in the vicinity. To combat this problem bells were rung at a certain time in the evening, depending on the season, as a sign to *coverfeu* (Old French) 'to cover' or smother the fire. This practice of the ringing of bells to signal a sanction or obedience to a civic order gradually developed into the modern word curfew. In its current form, a curfew concerns a stated time when people must return to their houses and not be on the streets. Ironically, what happens when the curfew is called and someone returns to their place of abode to find it on fire?

> *After Danny had been caught getting into trouble with his friends in the park, his parents imposed a strict curfew.*

330 **Edacious**

ADJECTIVE

Originally relating to having an extraordinarily large appetite, edacious has developed as an alternative to voracious, describing a seemingly insatiable need to consume something.

> *My wife has an edacious appetite for trashy television soap operas.*

331 Eunoia

NOUN

A beautiful word in print but a potential banana skin in speech as nobody is entirely sure exactly how it should be pronounced (which probably accounts for its rarity). Eunoia is thought to have been coined by the Greek philosopher Aristotle, who uses the word to describe the warmness of feeling between spouses essential for a balanced and happy life. However, Roman politician and philosopher Cicero uses the word to describe benevolence and kindness. A modern interpretation of the word is the ability to display calmness and balance in speech and thought, especially when speaking in front of an audience. The argument regarding how the word is pronounced centres on how many syllables should be voiced, either three ('u-noy-er') or four ('u-no-e-er'). Either way, an elegant word expressing an elegant concept, which is also the shortest word in the English language to contain all five vowels.

> *The speech captivated the audience with its natural sense of eunoia.*

332 Tawdry

ADJECTIVE

In the seventh century, Etheldreda, one of five daughters of Anna, King of the East Angles, abandoned her husband and her royal position to become a nun. She entered a convent and formed an abbey at Ely in Cambridgeshire at the site where Ely Cathedral stands to this day. Etheldreda, aka St Audrey, was celebrated for her saintliness and piety and, according to St Bede, died of a tumour in her throat, which she took as a punishment for her vanity in wearing necklaces in her youth. Her shrine became a principal site of pilgrimage in England and an annual fair was held in her honour at Ely on 17 October, St Audrey's Day. At these fairs, various kinds of cheap novelties and supposed religious artefacts were on sale, including a type of necklace called St Audrey's lace, which by the seventeenth century became 'tawdry lace'. Eventually, tawdry came to be used to describe anything inexpensive and kitsch. The word also has an extended sense to mean anything pretty shabby or unpalatable, which seems harsh on St Audrey, who by all accounts was a thoroughly good egg and not the least bit tawdry.

The tawdry details of the affair were leaked to the tabloid press.

333 Lade

VERB

The verb 'to lade' is rare in that it is used most commonly in its adjectival form 'laden'. In the sixteenth century, a 'lade' (noun) referred to goods and/or something to be transported that was heavy and cumbersome. Only the adjective has really survived in regular usage, as in somebody 'laden with problems and issues'.

The donkeys were laden with heavy packs for the climb up the mountain.

334 Assassin

NOUN

John Wilkes Booth, Sirhan Sirhan, Lee Harvey Oswald, Mark Chapman and Gavrilo Princip are arguably the most notorious assassins in modern history – although there is little evidence that any of them ever took drugs. The origins of the word assassin come from Medieval Latin *assassinus* from Arabic *ḥashshāshīn*, plural of *ḥashshāsh*, meaning 'a worthless person', or quite literally a hashish user/dope smoker. Conspiracy theorists put forth ideas that Oswald and Sirhan were brainwashed or manipulated in some way – either via hypnosis or psychotronics – however, western European crusaders believed the original assassins to be very much off their rockers. The Arabic name derives from the cult of Hassan i-Sabbah, a sort of eleventh-century version of either Osama Bin-Laden or the Ayatollah Khomeini, who preached a fundamentalist form of the Islamic faith and would dispatch his *ḥashshāshīn* (assassins) from his mountain hideaway to murder and carry out various heinous atrocities. It is rather depressing to think that a thousand years have passed since Hassan i-Sabbah's reign of terror and nothing much has changed for the better. The word is thought to have entered English through French due to a rumour that Richard I (aka Lionheart) had made a pact with Hassan's followers to travel to Europe and assassinate the King of France.

> *The assassins of Hassan i-Sabbah were feared throughout the medieval world.*

335 Farce

NOUN

The term farce is derived from the French word for 'stuffing', in reference to actors improvising extra scenes in medieval religious dramas. Later forms of this drama were performed as comical interludes during the fifteenth and sixteenth centuries. The oldest surviving farce may be *Le Garçon et l'Aveugle* (*The Boy and the Blind Man*) from after 1266, although the earliest farces that can be dated come from between 1450 and 1550. The best-known is *La Farce de Maître Pathelin* (*The Farce of Master Pathelin*) from *circa* 1460. When the word *farce* first appeared in English, it had to do with cookery, not comedy. In the fourteenth century, English adopted the word from Middle French, retaining its original meaning of 'forcemeat' or 'stuffing'. In modern usage, farce has developed a secondary meaning of a situation that has descended into laughable chaos.

> *The 'weekend service' on the railways is a complete farce; nobody has a clue what is going on.*

⌒⌒⌒

336 Talent

NOUN

Talent derives from the Greek word *talanton*, which referred to a unit of weight or sum of money. Latin used the word to mean 'a will to do something' and so when it first appeared in English in the thirteenth century it took on the meaning of an inclination or hunger to achieve. One of Jesus's parables tells of the three servants entrusted money (talents) by their master – two invest the money and make a profit, one buries his in the earth for safe-keeping – a classic case of wasted talent.

Everyone knew she was a gifted artist but she gave it all up – what a waste of a talent.

∽

337   Quixotic

ADJECTIVE

The eponymous hero of Miguel de Cervantes' Spanish novel *El Ingenioso Hidalgo Don Quijote de la Mancha* (1605) – better known in English as *Don Quixote* – provides the root for this word. The adjective quixotic is based on his name and has been used to describe unrealistic idealists since at least the early eighteenth century. The novel has given English other words as well. *Dulcinea,* the name of Quixote's beloved, has come to mean mistress or sweetheart, and *rocinante,* which is sometimes used to refer to an old, broken-down horse, comes from the name of the hero's less-than-gallant steed. *Don Quixote* was hugely popular and remains the most translated book in the world after the Bible. The English idiomatic expression (dating from seventeenth century) 'tilting at windmills' derives from one of the most memorable passages in the book when the deluded knight attacks a windmill thinking it to be a giant and means 'to fight imaginary enemies'.

His quixotic behaviour has become a cause of concern recently; I think he might be bi-polar.

∽

338 **Plebiscite**

NOUN

Deriving from the Latin *plebis scitum*, which was a law voted by decree of the common people, plebiscite means a vote whereby the inhabitants of an entire country or district can choose for or against a proposal or on a choice of government or leader. The derogatory term 'pleb', as in someone of limited education or culture, is derived from the French *plebe*, meaning 'common person'.

There is to be a plebiscite to elect a new mayor.

339 **Savant**

NOUN

Savant derives from Latin *sapere*, meaning 'to be wise', and comes via Middle French *savoir*, meaning 'to know'. The modern meaning in English, however, is much more complex and often relates to someone who exhibits extraordinary brilliance in a particular field of knowledge, typically mathematics or science, but often struggles with the more routine, everyday aspects of general knowledge and understanding. In this sense the somewhat cruel expression 'idiot savant' emerged, to describe a condition which is often closely, and more politely, linked with the autistic spectrum.

The film Rain Man *details the relationship between two brothers, one a chancer of dubious morality and the other an autistic but highly gifted mathematical savant.*

340 Simulacrum

NOUN

Closely linked to the word simulation (both words derive from the Latin *simulare*, meaning 'to copy'), simulacrum is an artificial representation of something real. Originally, the word related to direct copies, such as waxwork figures or portrait paintings, but over time it has come to be seen as a negative and artificial replacement for something. Post-Structuralist philosophers such as Jean Baudrillard and Jacques Derrida adopted the phrase to describe the artificiality of modern cultural forms.

> *Reality TV is the ultimate, if oxymoronic, simulacrum of real life.*

341 Innocuous

ADJECTIVE

The addition of a prefix in latinate words gives you the clue as to exactly the definition. The Latin verb *nocēre*, which means 'to harm' or 'to injure', provides the origin for innocuous – something not to be afraid of as it is basically harmless. Innocuous has, however, developed a subtle secondary negative meaning when applied to things that are basically useless or quite pathetic and lame. This is a shame as in an increasingly hostile world anything benign and innocuous is to be welcomed.

> *Despite all the anticipation, the publication of the report highlighted mostly innocuous details.*

342   Trenchant

ADJECTIVE

In Anglo-French the verb *trencher* held the meaning of 'to cut' or 'scythe'. A sense of something 'cutting' prevailed in to English, first through the military, where a trenchant sword was one that was sharpened. Eventually, the word came to be used to describe people with a particularly cutting manner in social situations – think Dorothy Parker or Oscar Wilde, both of whom had trenchant personality traits.

> *It was an awkward moment when she met her ex-husband at the party, but she felt she held her own with some trenchant remarks.*

343   Chauvinism

NOUN

During the Napoleonic Wars, French soldier Nicolas Chauvin was seriously injured, and although he received a pension, he remained poor and disabled. Despite his misfortune, Chauvin was a fanatical supporter of Napoleon and continued to support the deposed emperor long after Napoleon had been exiled. Oddly, one soldier's blind devotion to an unpopular cause or ideology has come over time to mean total intransigence and a generally negative description of somebody who is stubborn and possibly out of touch with their social and political views – a chauvinist.

> *The comments made during the television debate revealed the candidate's rampant chauvinism.*

344 Verbiage

NOUN

An ironic inclusion to the entries in this book. Verbiage derives from French (via Old French) and means 'to chatter or ramble in speech or writing'. There is often a negative connotation to the use of the term, as someone guilty of verbiage uses far too many words, often in a superfluous and/or pretentious manner.

> *He liked to hold court at dinner parties but was oblivious to the fact that his verbiage made him seem tedious and dull.*

345 Vicarious

ADJECTIVE

A word that can be used in various contexts. To experience something vicariously is usually to gain pleasure from observing or receiving information about another person's actions and behaviour. However, an alternative meaning is to replace another person in a particular action or situation or, in the case of vicarious punishment, to be held to account for another's actions. The controversial legal ruling of joint enterprise is an illustration of vicarious punishment. For example, two people are robbing a bank, one person shoots and kills a security guard but both the robbers are charged with murder even though only one person fired the gun. A further context for vicarious is in the delegation of authority or, put simply, asking another person to make decisions on your behalf.

> *The men in the bar derived vicarious pleasure from the wild tales of the landlord's sexual exploits.*

346 Maverick

NOUN

The original Maverick was a nineteenth century Texan lawyer named Samuel A. Maverick. In lieu of a longstanding debt, Maverick was given 400 cattle but as he had no interest in being a cowboy, he left the livestock more or less to roam free. His indolence – or more plausibly his disinterest in matters of farming – resulted in none of his cattle being branded, which led local rival ranch owners to begin stealing his herd and branding them as their own. Samuel Maverick eventually realized the error of his ways and sold both the remaining cattle and the ranch. His name, however, has become synonymous with an individual who wilfully does things by their own rules and doesn't follow accepted convention.

He likes to pretend he's something of a maverick but when push comes to shove he falls into line.

347 Plaudit

NOUN

Valete et plaudite is a common phrase found at the end of classical tragedies and is an exhortation to the audience that translates as 'give us your applause'. The word derives from the Latin verb *plaudere*, 'to applaud', and when it first entered into English it was pronounced in its original Latin form as a three-syllable noun, although gradually over time the 'e' became silent and finally disappeared from the spelling. Although up until the nineteenth century if one received plaudits it meant one was applauded, in modern usage it refers to any form of critical praise.

Her performance has received considerable plaudits from critics and audiences.

348 Matutolypea

NOUN

Do you wake up some days under a cloud? Do you have times when it seems the whole world is weighing down on you and you find yourself being snappy and grumpy with everyone and everything? Well, then you have suffered from matutolypea – the state of being bad-tempered in the mornings. The word is an odd hybrid of the Roman *Matuta*, the goddess of the dawn, and the Greek word *lype*, used in the sense of grief or sorrow. The English expression 'got out of bed on the wrong side' is the closest definition of matutolypea.

> *I suffer from acute matutolypea, especially on Monday mornings on the way to work.*

349 Deadline

NOUN

A good friend of mine, the author and mathematician Chris Maslanka, once explained to me the concept of 'hard' and 'soft' deadlines. The former, according to Chris, were unavoidable and immovable; the latter had considerable wriggle room and were merely indicative (I'm hoping my editor somehow misses this entry). The original meaning of deadline, however, was extremely harsh – in fact, terminally so. In the American Civil War (1861–5), the deadline was a line, usually in the form of a small trench, approximately five metres from the inner perimeter fence of a prisoner-of-war camp. Any prisoner who crossed this line, even unwittingly, was immediately shot on suspicion of attempting to escape. Deadlines then entered into publishing jargon, first to mean the guideline on the bed of cylinder printing presses over which type should not stray and, eventually, figuratively to mean the point in time by which all copy needed to be submitted for publication. In modern usage, deadlines are everywhere, from submitting tax returns to legal appeals and paying off debts.

> *I'm hopeless with deadlines but they are a necessary nuisance otherwise I'd never get this book finished.*

350 Callipygian

ADJECTIVE

This word sounds like it has been made up on the fly or perhaps is a modern pseudo-word cobbled together for no apparent purpose other than to show off, but in fact its first recorded use in English dates back to the 1830s. *Kalli* is a girl's name of Greek origin that translates as 'the fairest and most beautiful'. *Pygē* is the Greek word for backside. In English, therefore, to be described as callipygian is to be in possession of a pair of beautifully shaped buttocks.

> *Kylie Minogue is renowned for her petite stature and callipygian figure.*

351 Perambulate

VERB

Perambulate is formed from the Latin prefix *per-*, meaning 'through', and *ambulare,* meaning 'to walk'. The word was originally used in Scottish English to describe making an inspection of a piece of land on foot for the purposes of providing a survey. Later, in the eighteenth century, perambulators were invented to make it easier to transport infants and babies around (shortened now to 'prams'). To perambulate in modern usage is a rather highbrow word for taking a nice, pleasurable stroll.

> *We decided to perambulate the length of the causeway as the weather was so nice.*

❧

352 Filibuster

VERB/NOUN

A curious word of uncertain origin with various different meanings, filibuster is thought by some etymologists to have originally been a Dutch seafaring term borrowed into various languages. One of the original meanings of the word in Spanish (*filibustero*) related to pirates and buccaneers and the practice of raiding foreign territories and stealing plunder. The English language borrowed the term in the nineteenth century to describe American mercenaries making incursions into South American and Caribbean countries with the aim of inciting revolutions. By the late nineteenth century, the sense of political subterfuge transferred to legislative matters and 'to filibuster' became the term for deliberately delaying a vote or disrupting a political process, usually by giving long-winded speeches or submitting petty amendments and queries. The first known filibuster was Roman senator Cato the Younger (95–47 BC) who, in order to disrupt legislation he didn't agree with, would often give long speeches until the sun went down, as the Roman senate had to conduct all business before nightfall.

> *Having gained control of the house, the party is able to effectively filibuster any welfare reforms.*

❧

353 Dunce

NOUN

There is a strange irony behind the pejorative word dunce in that it derives from a very clever man, John Duns Scotus (1266–1308). 'The Subtle Doctor', as he was known, was one of the most influential philosophers and writers of the early Middle Ages. By the sixteenth century, Duns Scotus' influence in academia had started to fade and his devoted followers came to be regarded as reactionary and as objects of derision, summed up by the insulting nickname *dunsman*. To begin with a dunsman was a rather tiresome pedant but over time the meaning changed to describe somebody who is stupid. The dunce's cap was a particularly spiteful Victorian creation intended to inspire children to learning through fear of being made to wear a humiliating hat in class if they got something wrong.

> *John Duns Scotus was certainly no dunce; he was one of the most brilliant minds of his time.*

354 Etiquette

NOUN

The original definition of the French word *étiquette* was 'ticket' or 'label for identification' and this provided the root for the English word ticket. In Spanish, the word was appropriated and changed to *etiqueta* to mean a card of written protocols describing orders of antecedence and conduct issued to guests of the Spanish court. Over time, *etiqueta* came to be used for all ceremonies of established courts. The French court of Louis XVI embraced the idea of appropriate conduct and took the word *étiquette* back.

The English, although obsessed with manners, didn't adopt the word until much later during the eighteenth century.

The failure to reply to the invitation was a breach of common etiquette.

❧

355 Chthonic

ADJECTIVE

A word that is as tricky to pronounce as it is to spell correctly, chthonic derives from the Greek word *chthōn*, meaning 'the earth'. Anything chthonic (or less commonly chthonian) relates to what lies beneath the earth or, more literally, is a synonym for subterranean. Ancient Greek mythology abounds with tales of the underworld (*see* tantalize, p. 149), and of chthonic gods such as Hades and Persephone. The word is occasionally used in descriptions of shady crime lords and secret terrorist organizations.

In the new James Bond film, the master spy battles against SPECTRE, a shadowy and chthonic crime organization.

❧

356 Draconian

ADJECTIVE

Draco (*c.* 650–600 BC) was a legislator in Athens in Ancient Greece, who was charged by the people with drawing up a written code of law. Draco's Code was the first attempt at a written constitution in Athens, which up until this point had functioned on oral laws and blood feuds that were easily manipulated and corrupted by the Greek aristocracy. The code set out a series of harsh sanctions for criminal activities, most of which were punishable by the death penalty – even failure to pay debts could result in slavery. The adjective draconian doesn't necessarily relate to the death penalty but more generally any law or rule that decrees punishments that are excessively harsh or arguably unjust.

> *The sanctions for non-payment of parking fines set by the city council are positively draconian.*

༄

357 Declension

NOUN

In linguistics, declension is the inflection (changing the form of a word) of nouns, pronouns, adjectives and articles to indicate certain aspects such as number, gender or case. Shakespeare, however, coined a new meaning to the word in his play *Richard III* by using it to mean something suddenly deteriorating, in this case the reputation of a courtier after committing adultery. There is a rare subsidiary meaning of declension and that is 'a polite formal refusal'.

> *A beauty-waning and distressèd widow,*
> *Even in the afternoon of her best days,*
> *Made prize and purchase of his wanton eye,*
> *Seduced the pitch and height of his degree*
> *To base declension and loathed bigamy.*

WILLIAM SHAKESPEARE, *Richard III*, Act 3, Scene 1 (*c.* 1592)

༄

358 Placebo

NOUN

Placebo is Latin for 'I shall please', and for many centuries it was a phrase well known from religious services, specifically funerals, where it was common to recite Psalm 114 in the Vulgate, which contains the line: *Placebo Domino in regione vivorum* ('I shall please the Lord in the land of the living'). The medical usage of placebo is thought to date back to a quack London doctor from the seventeenth century who administered various dubious remedies (sweet syrups, fine-smelling ointments) more likely to please a patient than actually cure them; as a result he became known as Doctor Placebo. In modern usage, a placebo is a medicine or treatment administered to a patient that, although of limited effectiveness, is designed to stimulate a mental belief that it is a cure.

> *In drugs trials, pharmaceutical companies often substitute placebo pills in order to test data and effectiveness of different medicines.*

359 Jingoism

NOUN

'Hey jingo!' was a popular idiomatic expression often used by conjurors and magicians at the climax of a trick (a variant on 'hey presto'). 'By jingo' was also often used as a euphemism for 'by Jesus' to avoid blasphemy. During the Russian–Turkish war of 1877–8, the Prime Minister of Great Britain, Benjamin Disraeli (1804–81) advocated British military intervention in Turkey to protect Constantinople. The policy was not supported by the opposition Liberal party but had much popular appeal, as evidenced by a music hall ditty of the time: 'We don't want to fight, yet by jingo if we do, We've got the ships, we've got the men, We've got the money, too!' Someone who shared this strong patriotic belligerence became known as a jingo, and over time the word developed into the modern expression jingoism, meaning a rabid nationalistic sentiment.

The jingoism of the popular press during football World Cups is a national disgrace.

—

360 Minion

NOUN

A *filet mignon* is a common feature in bistros and brasseries in restaurants across the world. The phrase, although slightly pretentious, means 'dainty' or 'delicate' fillet – a small slice of (usually) beef steak. The French word *mignon* meaning 'darling or favourite' is the root of the term and this meaning for minion prevailed for several centuries. Gradually, however, the term minion developed a derogatory implication, meaning somebody subservient and inconsequential within an organization or corporation.

The governor filled the staff positions with his own cronies and minions.

—

361 Lambent

ADJECTIVE

Fire is often figuratively and descriptively expressed in terms of licking flames or tongues. Lambent derives from the Latin word *lambere*, meaning 'to lick', and describes something flickering or moving smoothly or lightly over a surface, or something shining softly and brightly. The word is also often associated with light and the exquisiteness of expression in writing or something that exudes a low but shining glow, as in the following lines from a poem by Alexander Pope:

> *Those smiling eyes, attemp'ring ev'ry ray,*
> *Shone sweetly lambent with celestial day.*

ALEXANDER POPE, *Eloisa to Abelard* (1717)

362 Palaver

NOUN

In the eighteenth century, it was common for Portuguese and English sailors to encounter each other during slave trading trips along the West African coast. The murky dealings of the slave trade involved much negotiation and the word for these was the Portuguese *palavra* meaning 'speech'. By the late nineteenth century, the meaning of palaver had taken on a negative connotation of a wearisome fuss or a tiresome task. The meaning of palaver as general chatter still survives but is rarely used these days.

> *I can make fresh mayonnaise but it's a bit of*
> *a palaver and easier just to buy a jar from the*
> *supermarket.*

363   Uncouth

ADJECTIVE

Uncouth derives from the Old English word *uncūth,* which is formed by the negative prefix *un-* with *cūth,* meaning 'familiar' or 'known'. Uncouth is an example of how a meaning of a word changes and in the process its original positive antonym disappears. How did a word that meant unfamiliar come to mean 'outlandish', 'graceless' or 'uncultivated'? This occurred over time as an expression of a fear of the unknown. Daniel Defoe in his novel *Captain Singleton* (1720) writes of hearing 'a strange noise more uncouth than any they had ever heard', and this sense of something mysterious and unknown prevailed for several centuries. Gradually, however, the term uncouth began to be applied to people's behaviour if it was strange and unfamiliar, and eventually to denote a general lack of social manners and rudeness.

> *It is uncouth to speak with your mouth full of food when eating.*

364   Cogent

ADJECTIVE

The Latin verb *agere,* which means 'to motivate' and 'to lead', provides the root for the adjective cogent. I shall endeavour to explain the word as cogently as I can. Cogent comes in to its own when trying to persuade or influence during a dispute or debate. A cogent argument is one with power that both motivates, inspires and ultimately 'leads' the discussion.

> *His impressive and cogent speech won the day at the University debating society.*

365 Serendipity

NOUN

In the mid-1700s, English writer and historian Horace Walpole, Fourth Earl of Orford (1717–97) stumbled upon an interesting tidbit of information while researching a work on heraldry. In a letter to his friend Horace Mann on 28 January 1754, he wrote: 'This discovery indeed is almost of that kind which I call Serendipity, a very expressive word, which as I have nothing better to tell you, I shall endeavour to explain to you: you will understand it better by the derivation than by the definition. I once read a silly fairy tale, called "The Three Princes of Serendip": as their highnesses travelled, they were always making discoveries, by accidents and sagacity, of things they were not in quest of . . .' The original fairy tale is thought to have been the work of an Italian writer and translator called Christoforo Armeno, who sourced the story from Oriental texts. The island that the three princes hail from is believed to be modern-day Sri Lanka, which was a stopping-off point for Arab sailors on the trade routes to China and is marked on Middle Eastern nautical maps as Sarandab or Serendip. Walpole's letter is the first known usage of the word, which retains its original meaning of discovering agreeable things by chance or happy coincidence.

Researching this book has entailed a good deal of serendipity when unearthing words with interesting origins and stories.

Index